Mandala Magic Zen Coloring Book

BY

BinxbyBooks.com

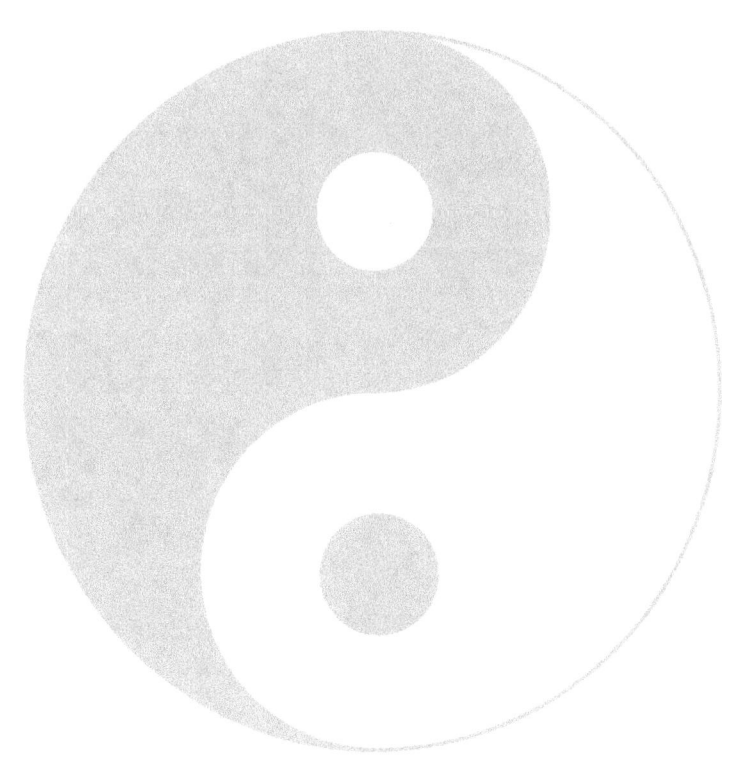

COPYRIGHT NOTICE

Mandala Magic Zen Coloring Book

Published by Binxby Books, PO Box 12031, Wichita, KS 67277-2031

Copyright © 2020 BinxbyBooks.com

All rights reserved. No portion of this book may be reproduced in any form without permission from the publisher, except as permitted by U.S. copyright law. For permissions contact:

support@binxbybooks.com

INTRODUCTION

This book contains 50 unique and calming Mandala style illustrations for coloring with custom zen messages for your enjoyment. We invite you to take your time and work on these pages as you are in the mood for a stress relieving and calming activity.

This coloring book can be used with markers, colored pencils, or crayons.

We appreciate you choosing this coloring book and hope it brings you peace and calm…

-Sincerely,
BinxbyBooks.com

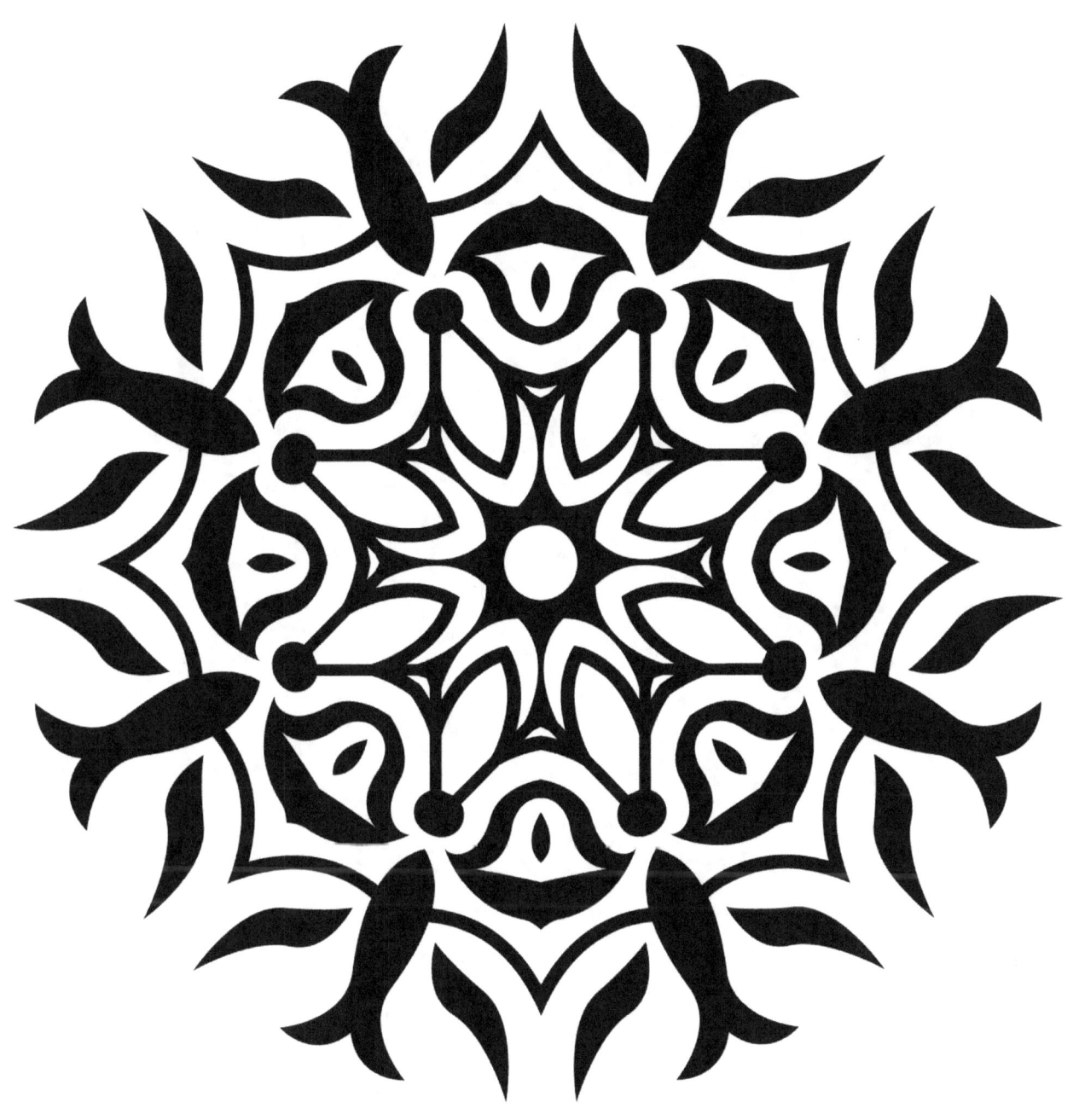

Doing what you like is freedom...liking what you do is happiness

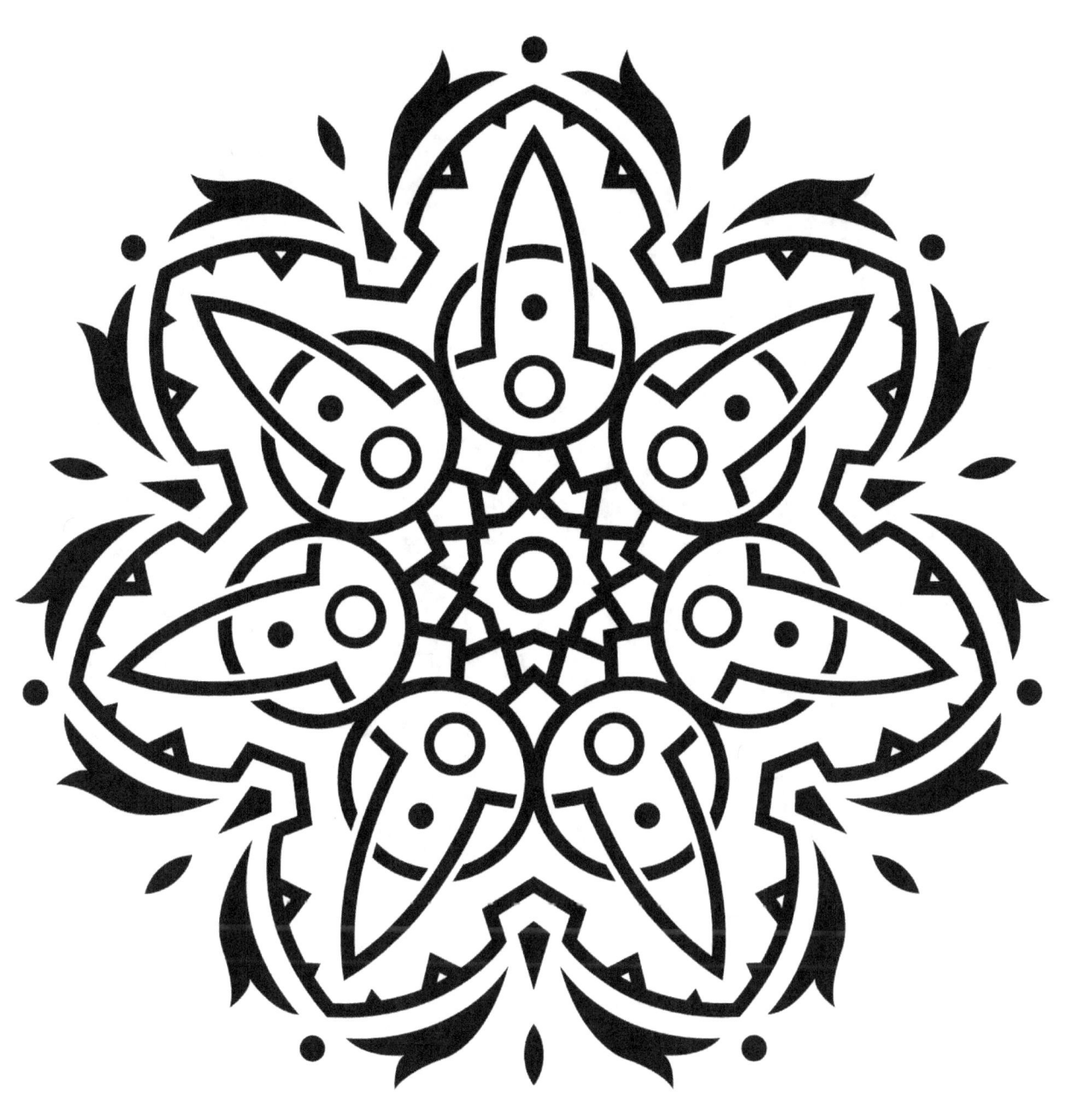

Be the change you want to see in the world

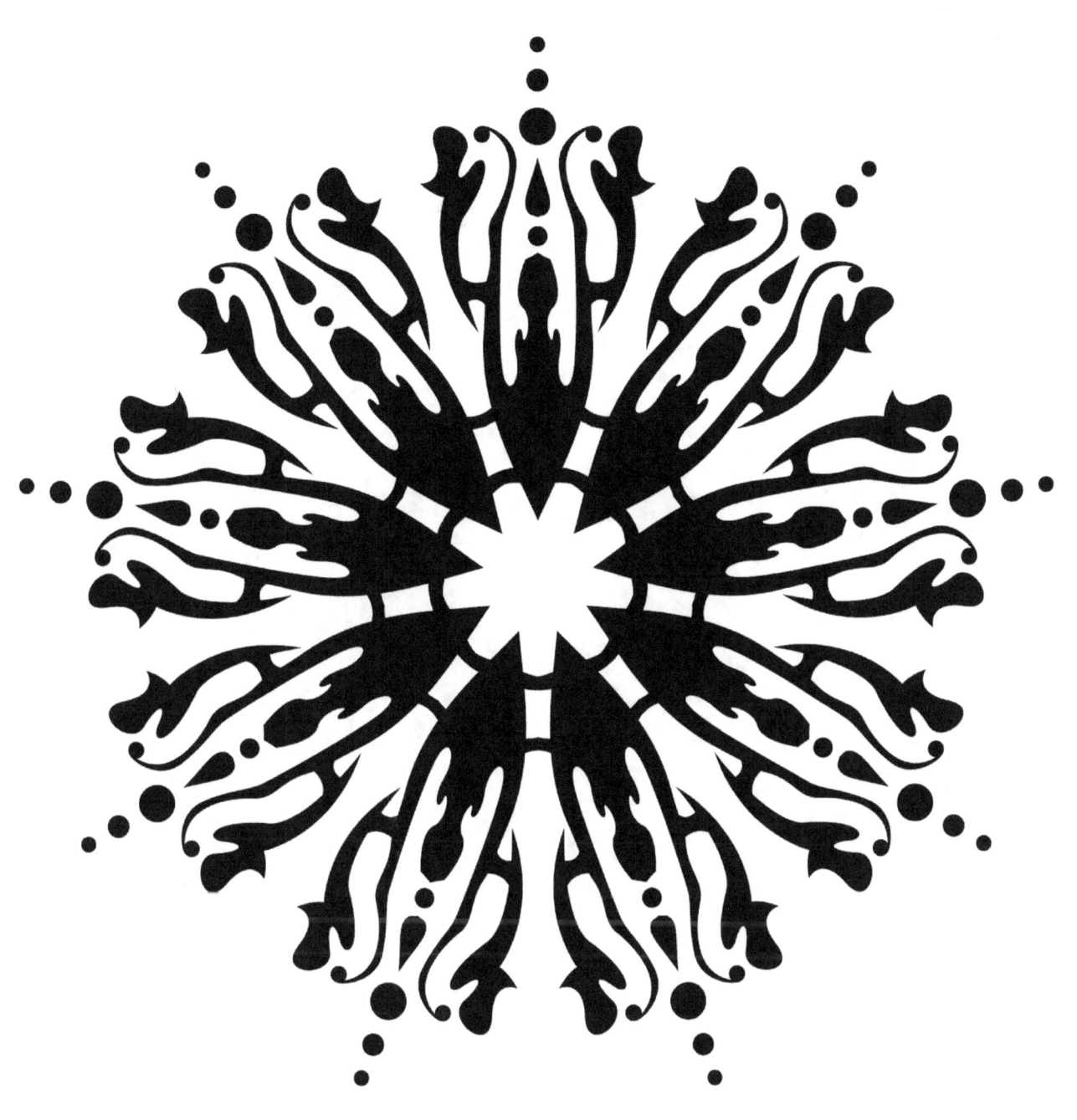

Health is wealth

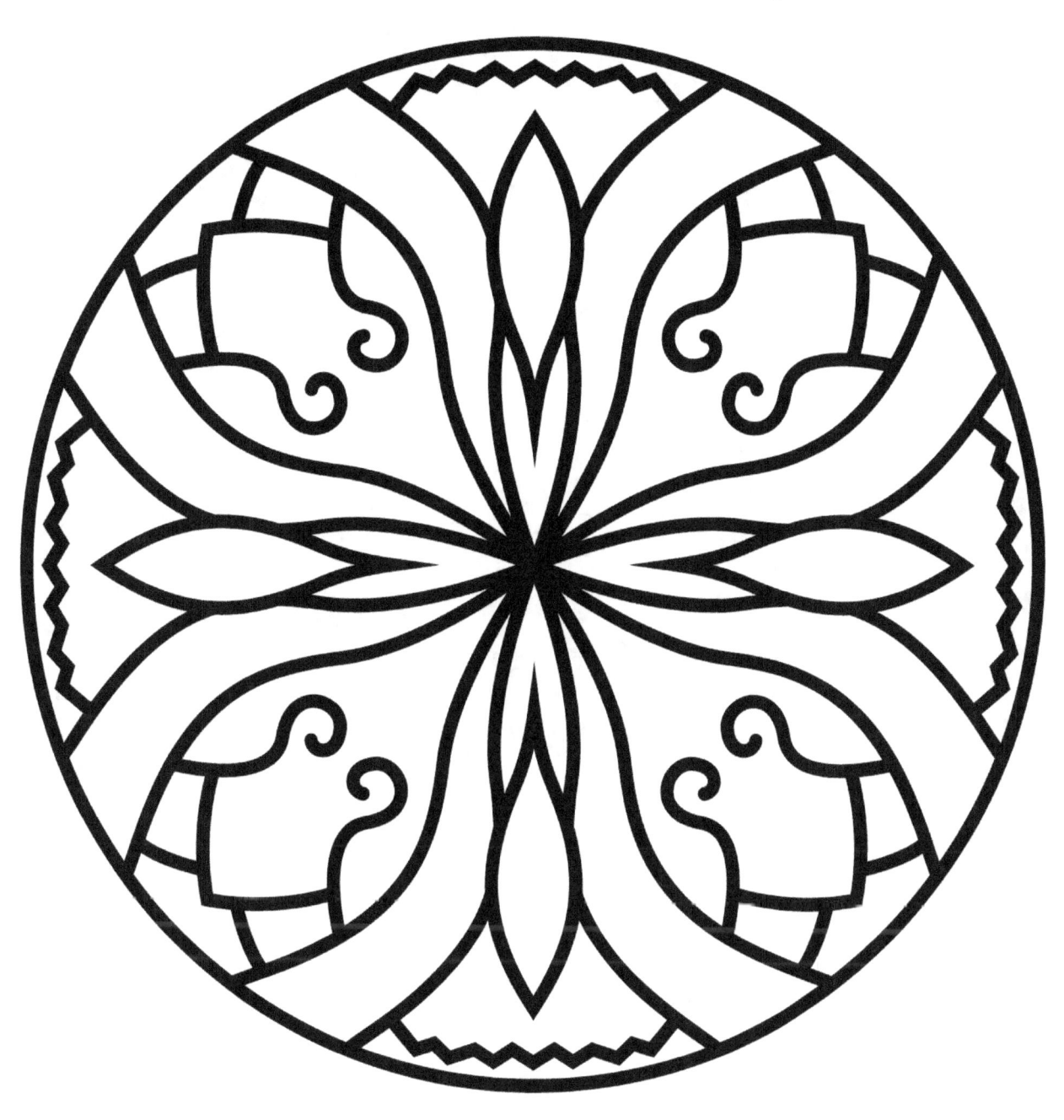

Move and the way will open

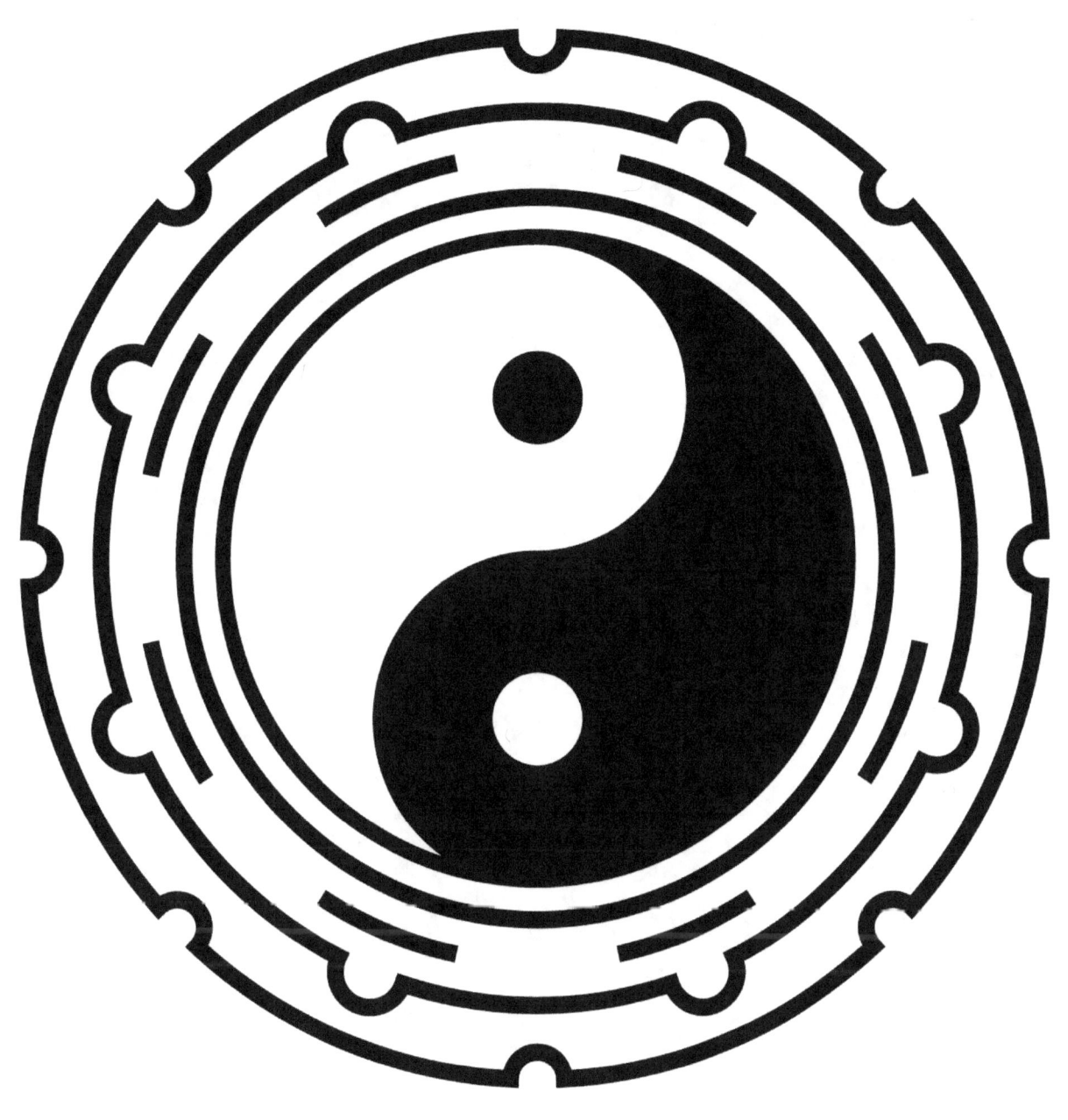

All that we are is the result of all that we have thought

14

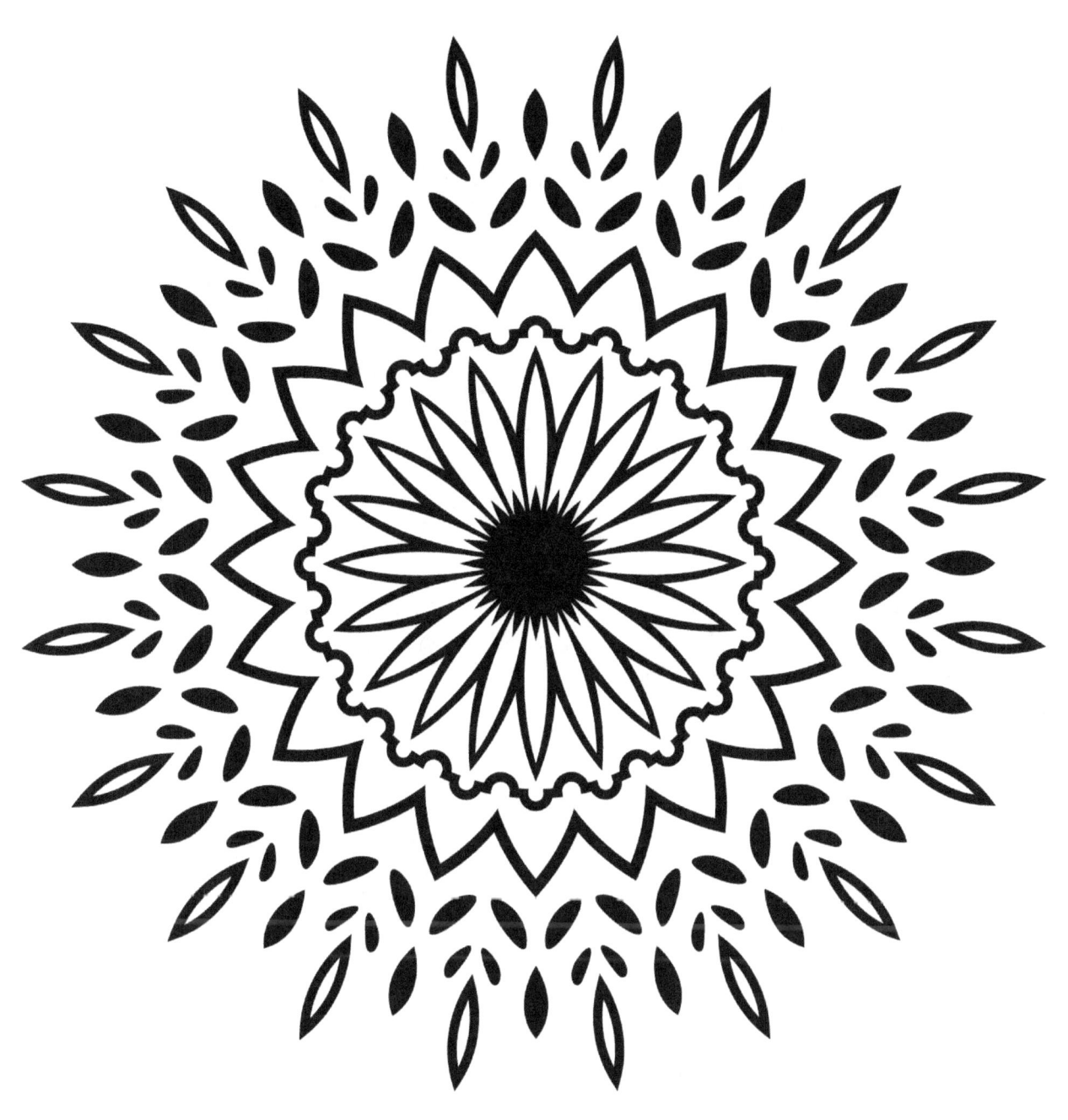

Always look on the bright side of life

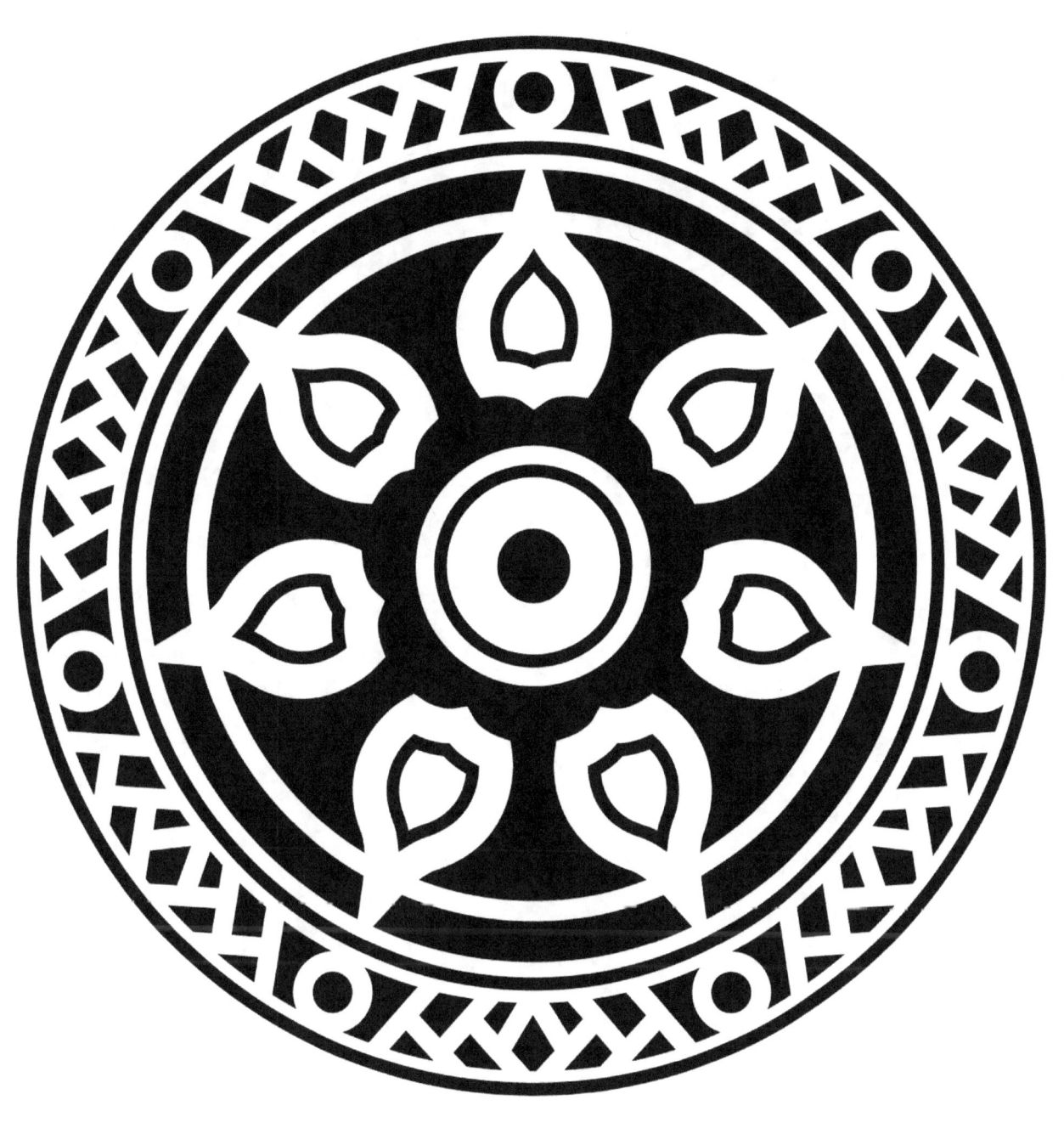

When the shoe fits, the foot is forgotten

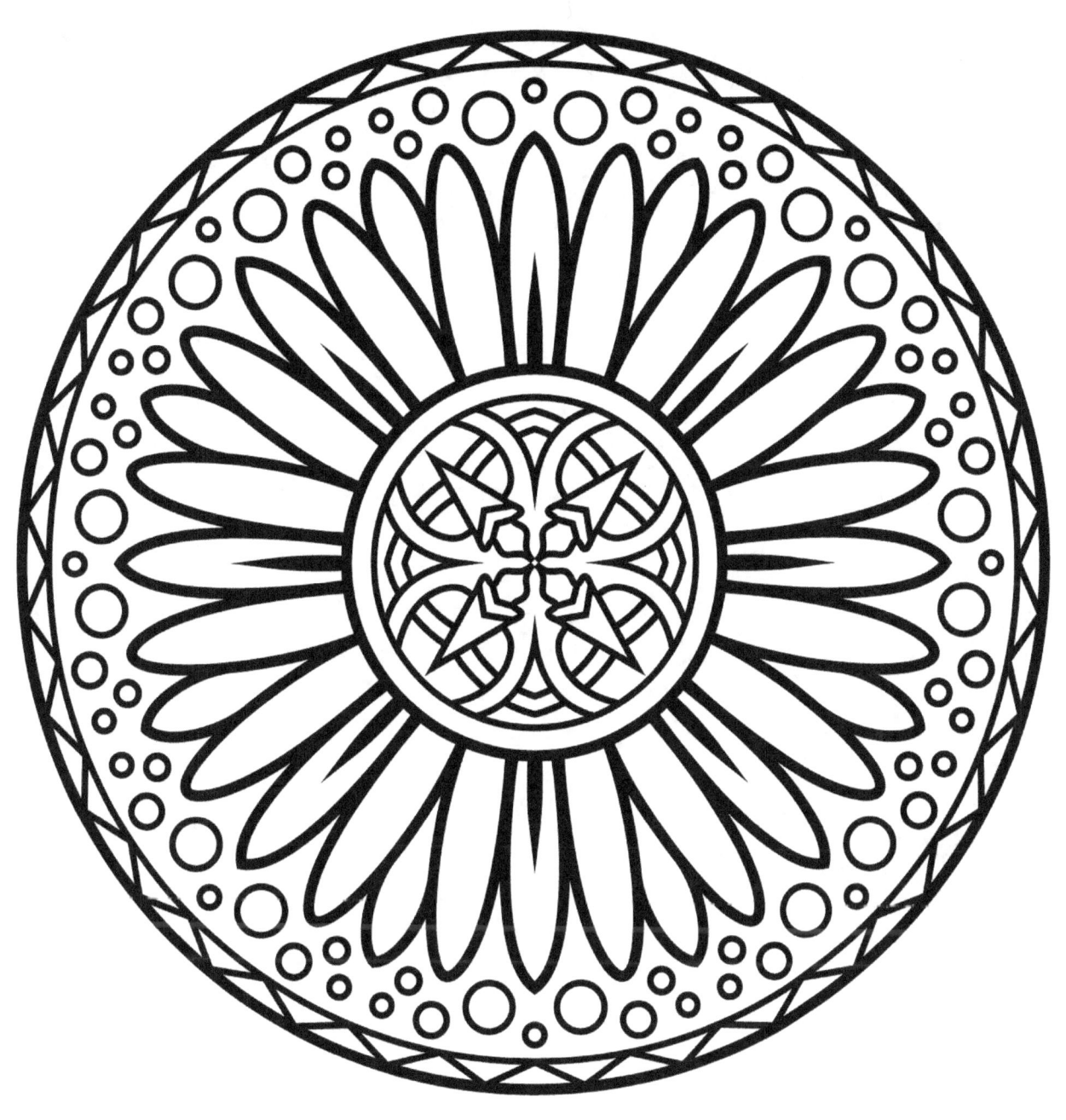

Negativity is a dark light we can shut off

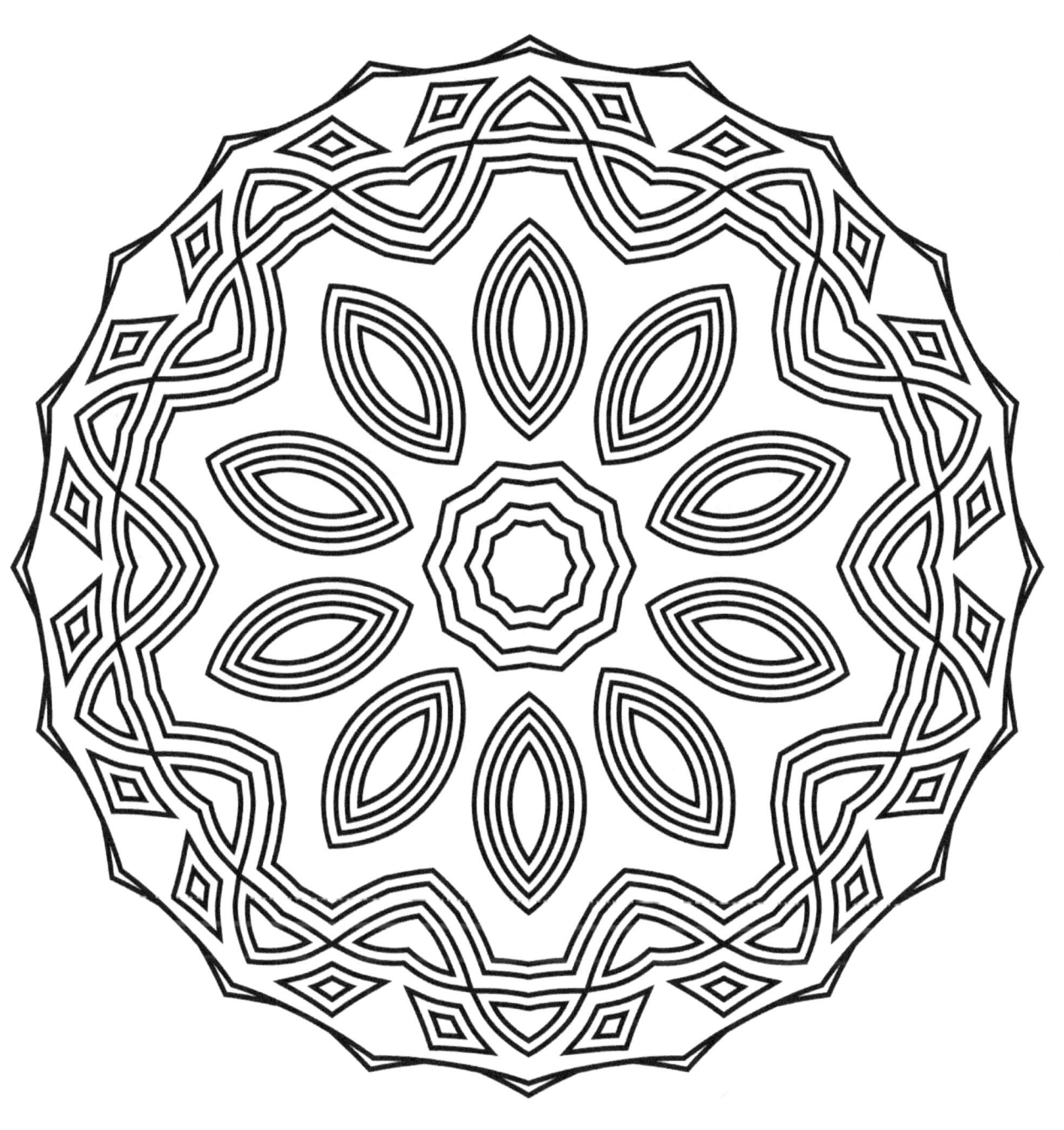

It is better to travel well than arrive

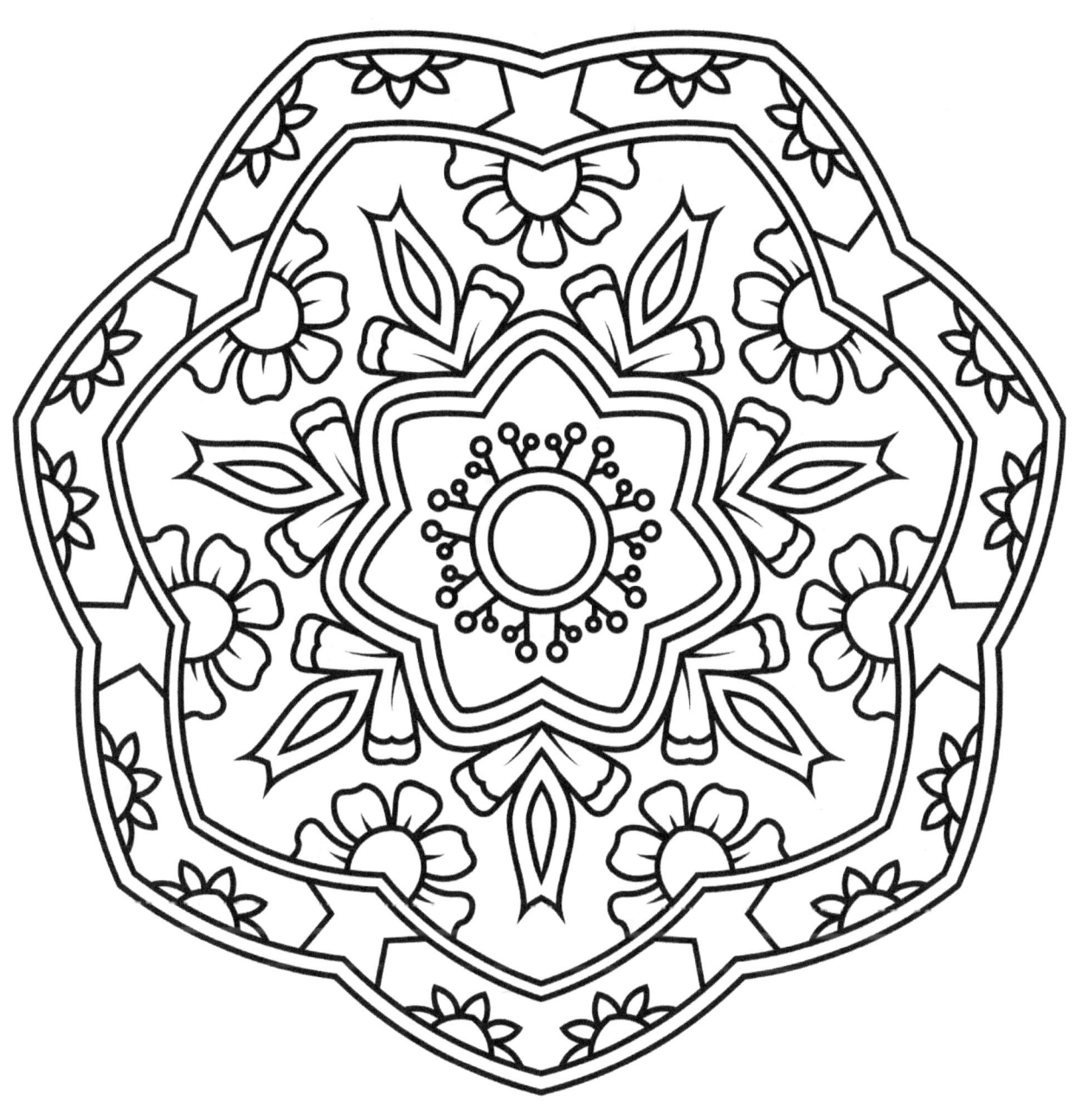

If anything is worth doing, do it with all your heart

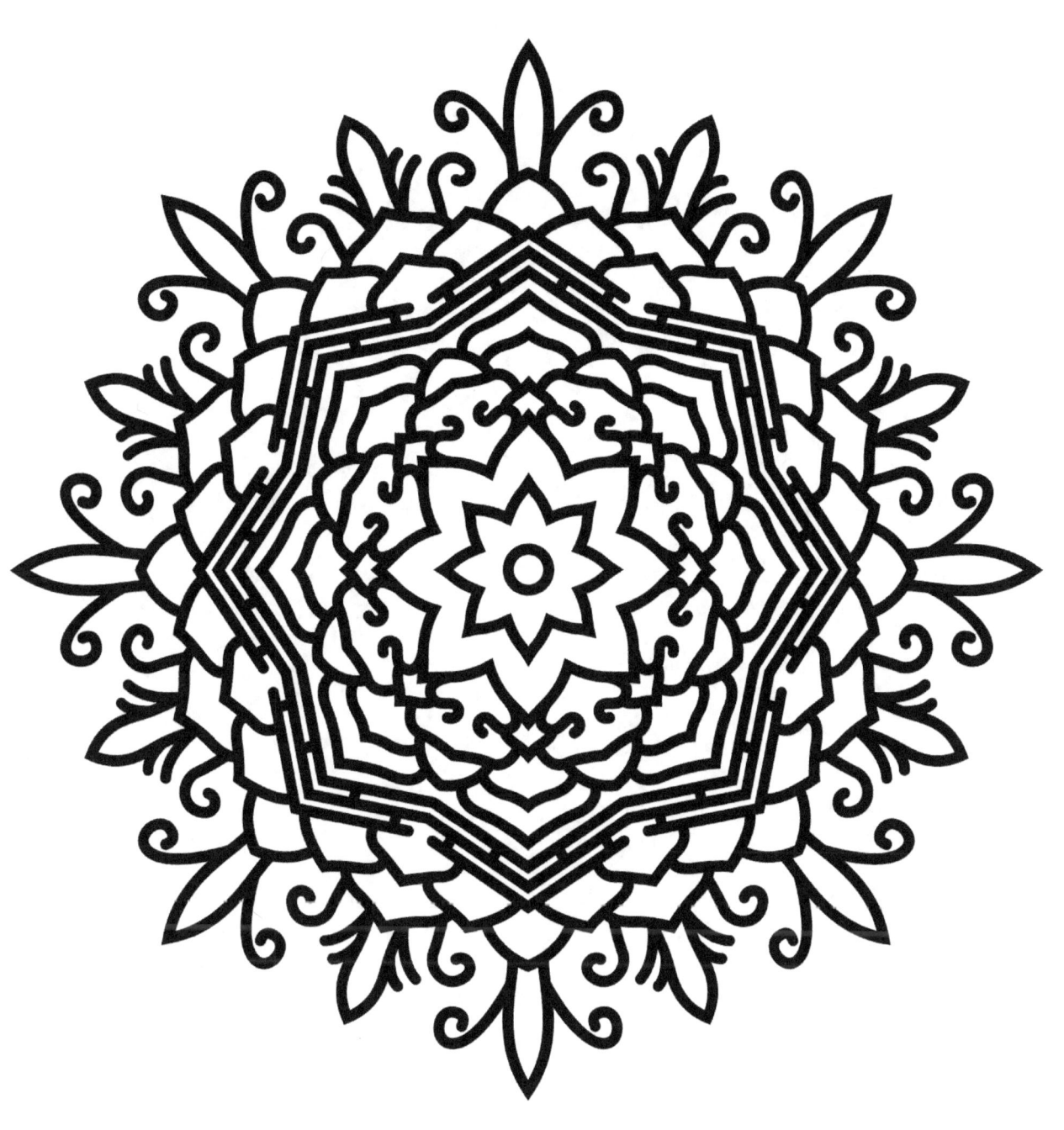

A disciplined mind brings happiness

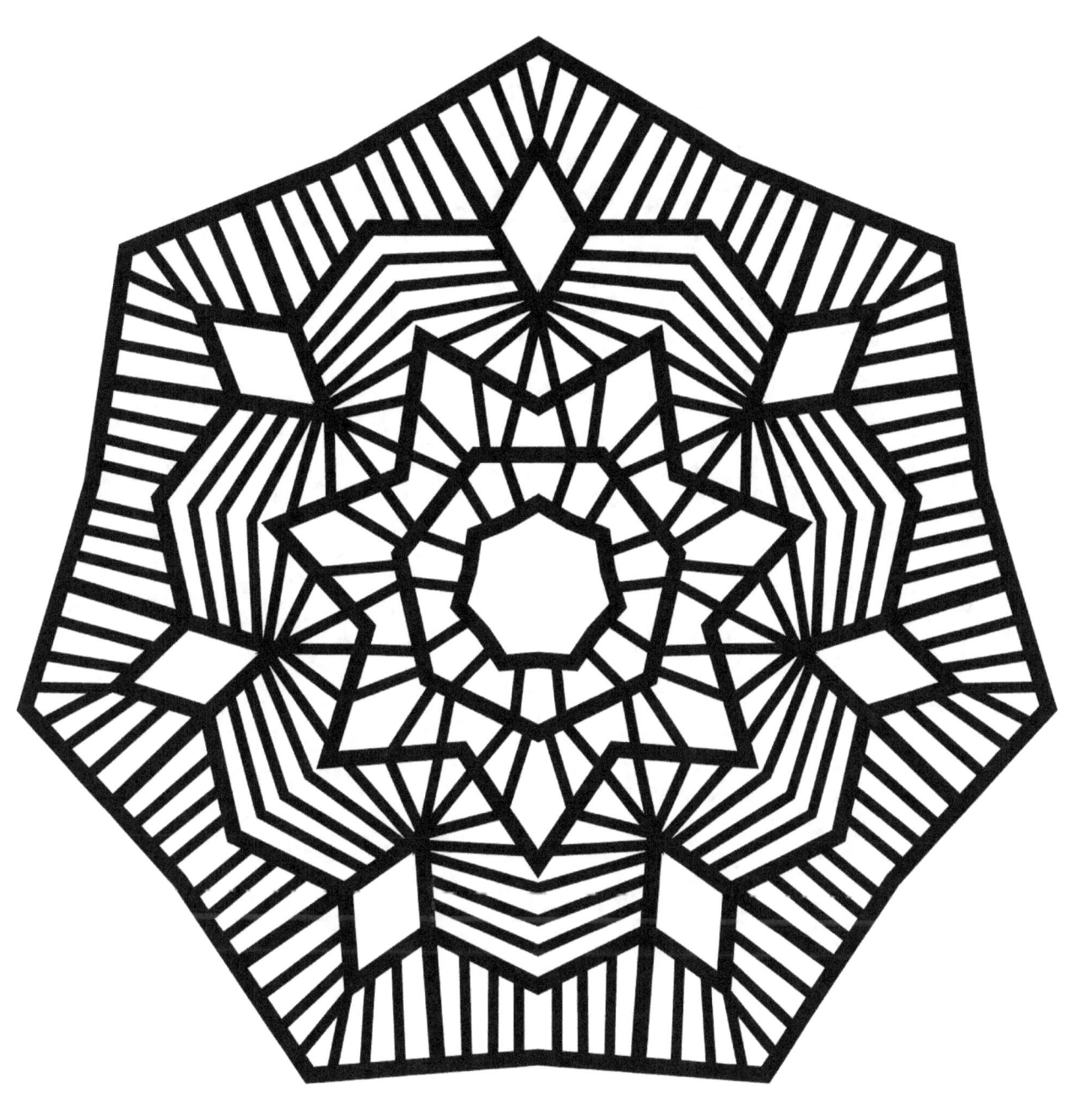

True love is born from understanding

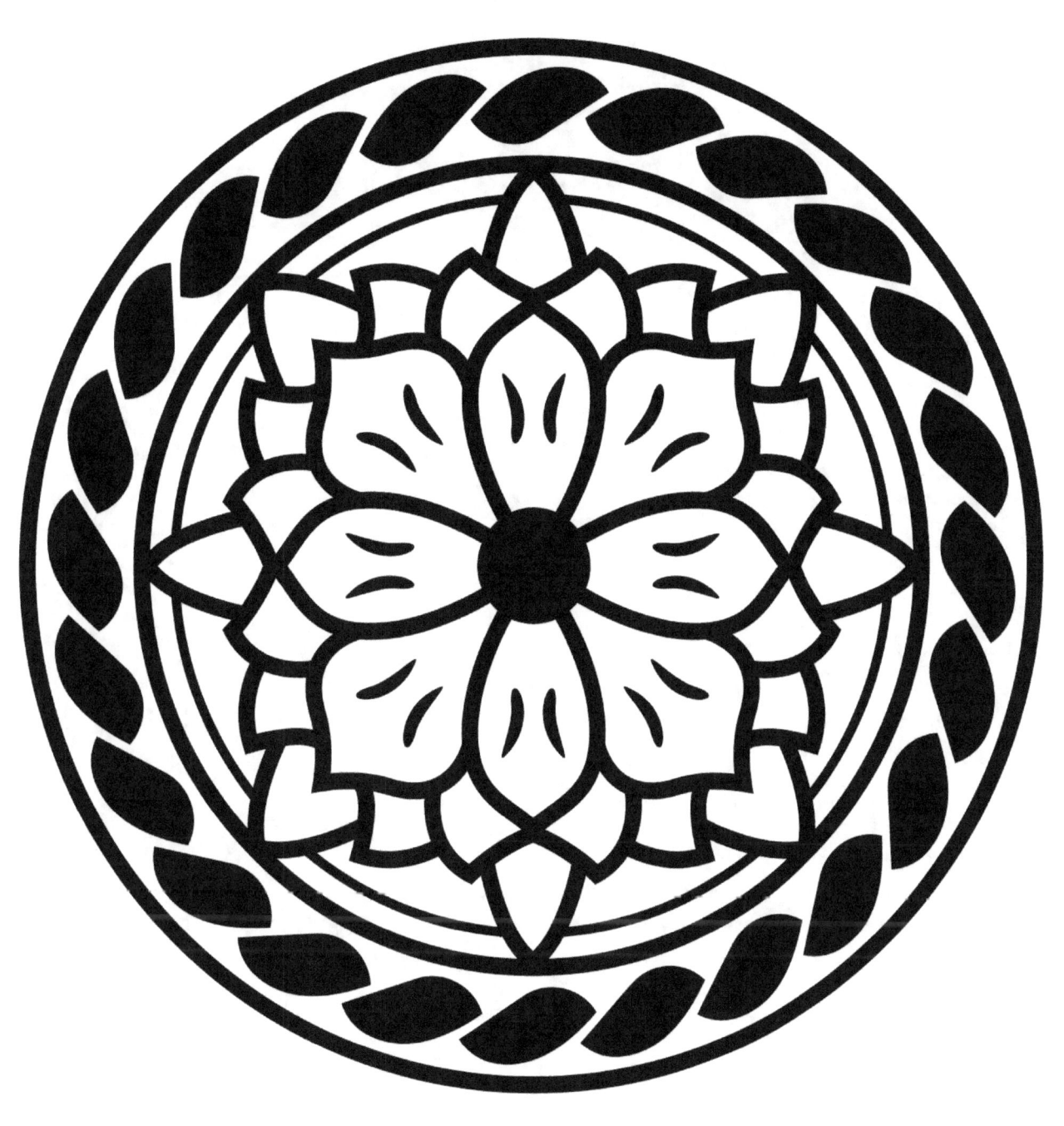

No snowflake ever falls in the wrong place

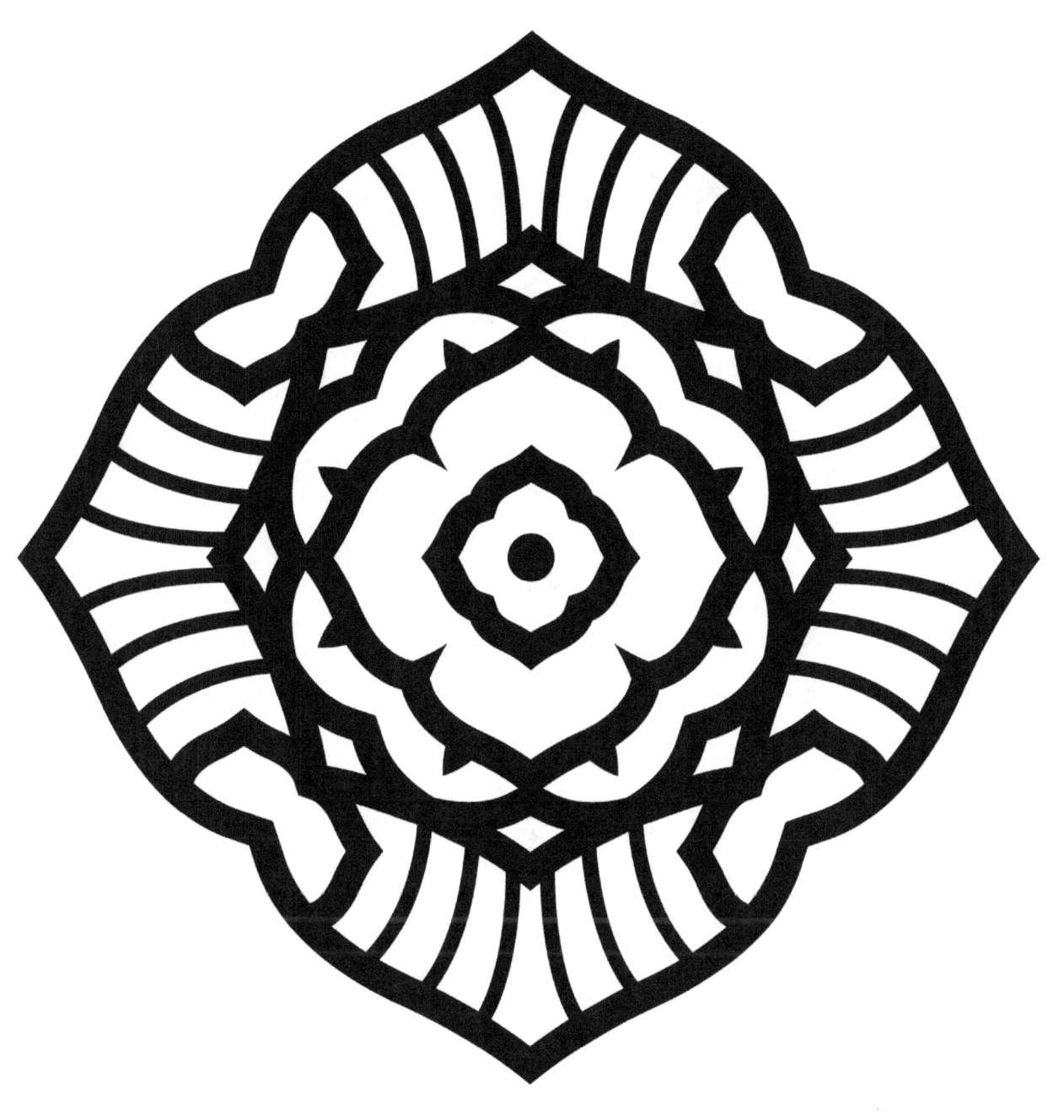

If you want to fly give up everything that weighs you down

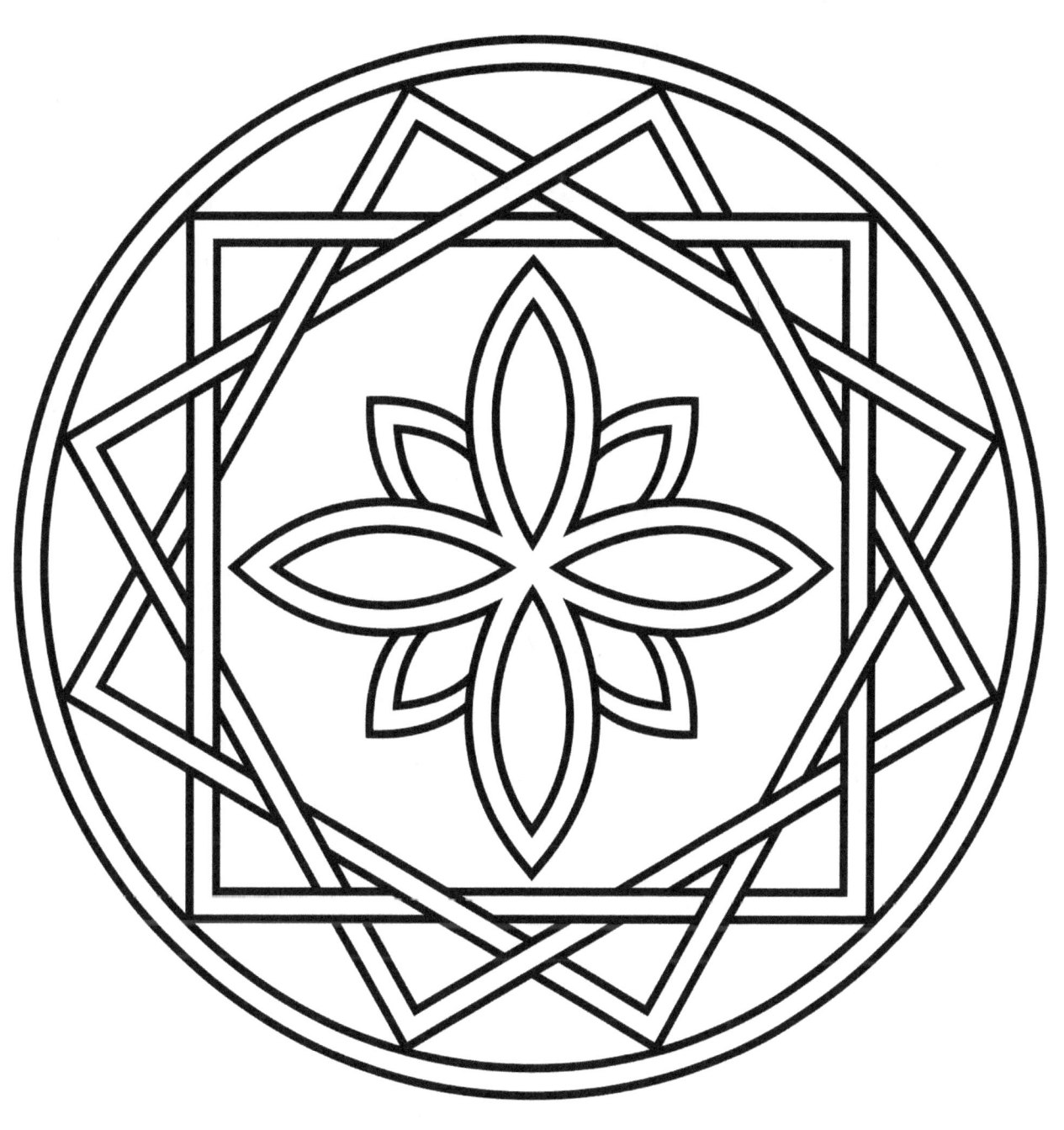

Words are the fog one has to see through

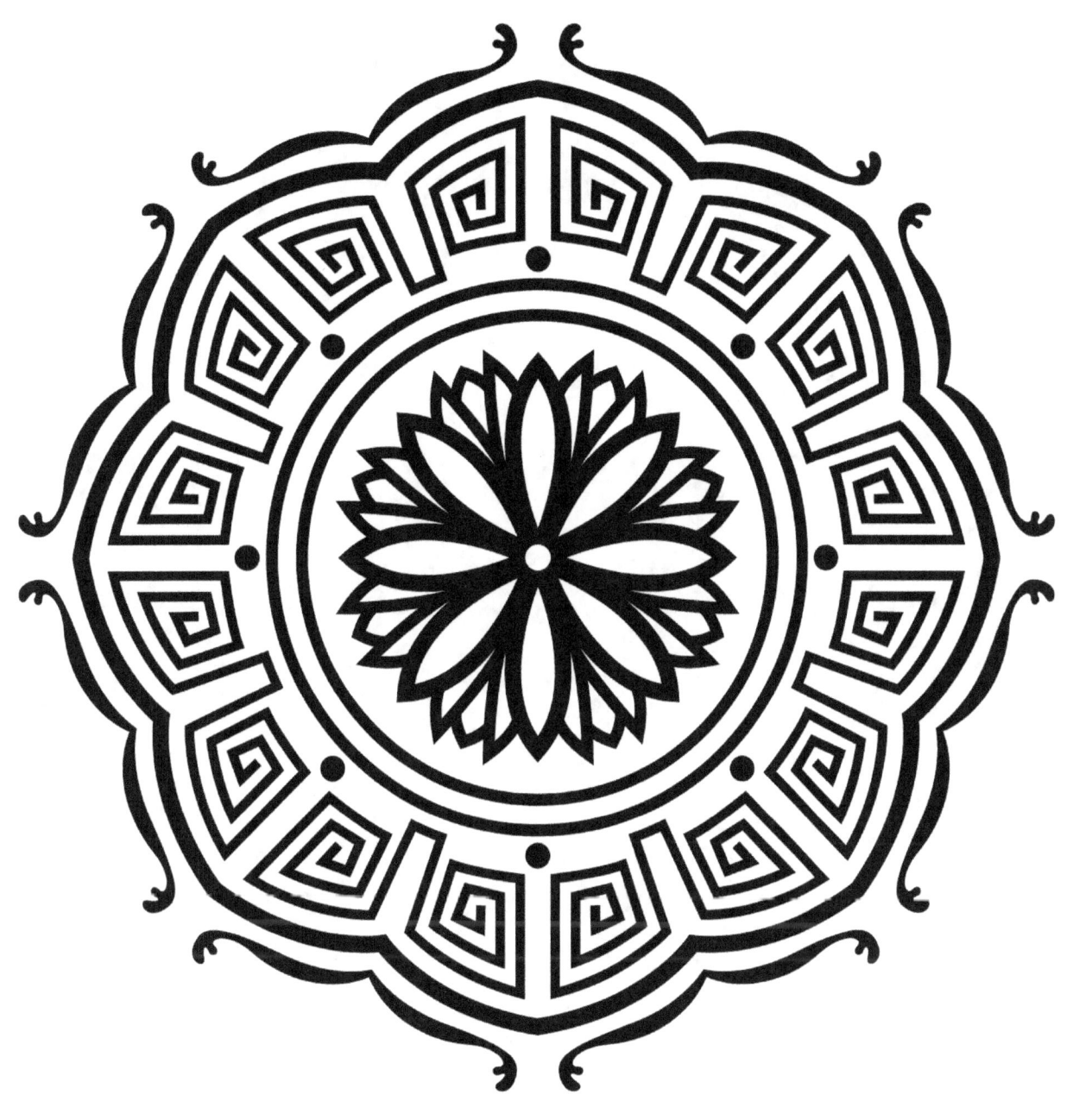

The opposite of a great truth is also true

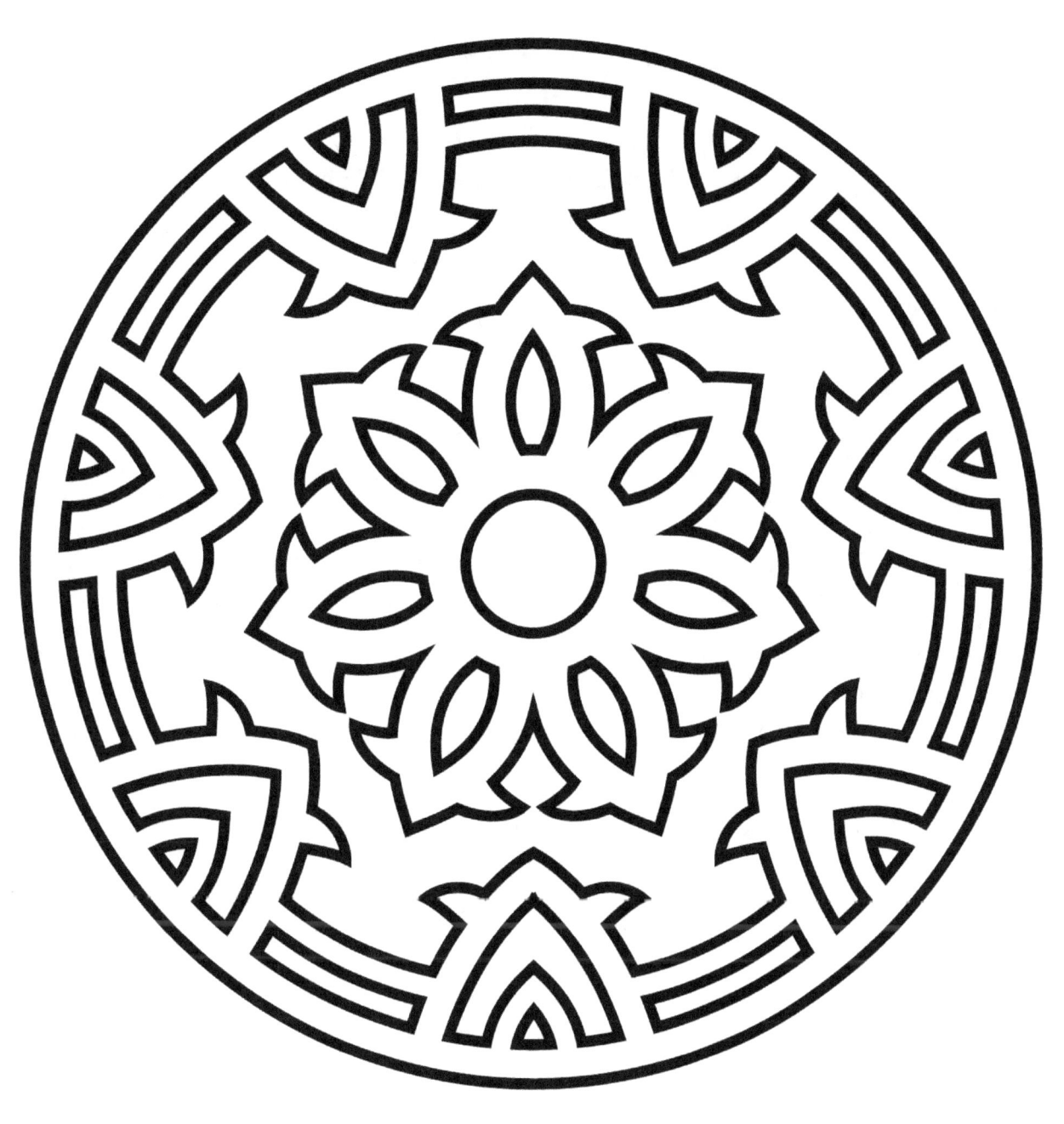

You only lose what you cling to

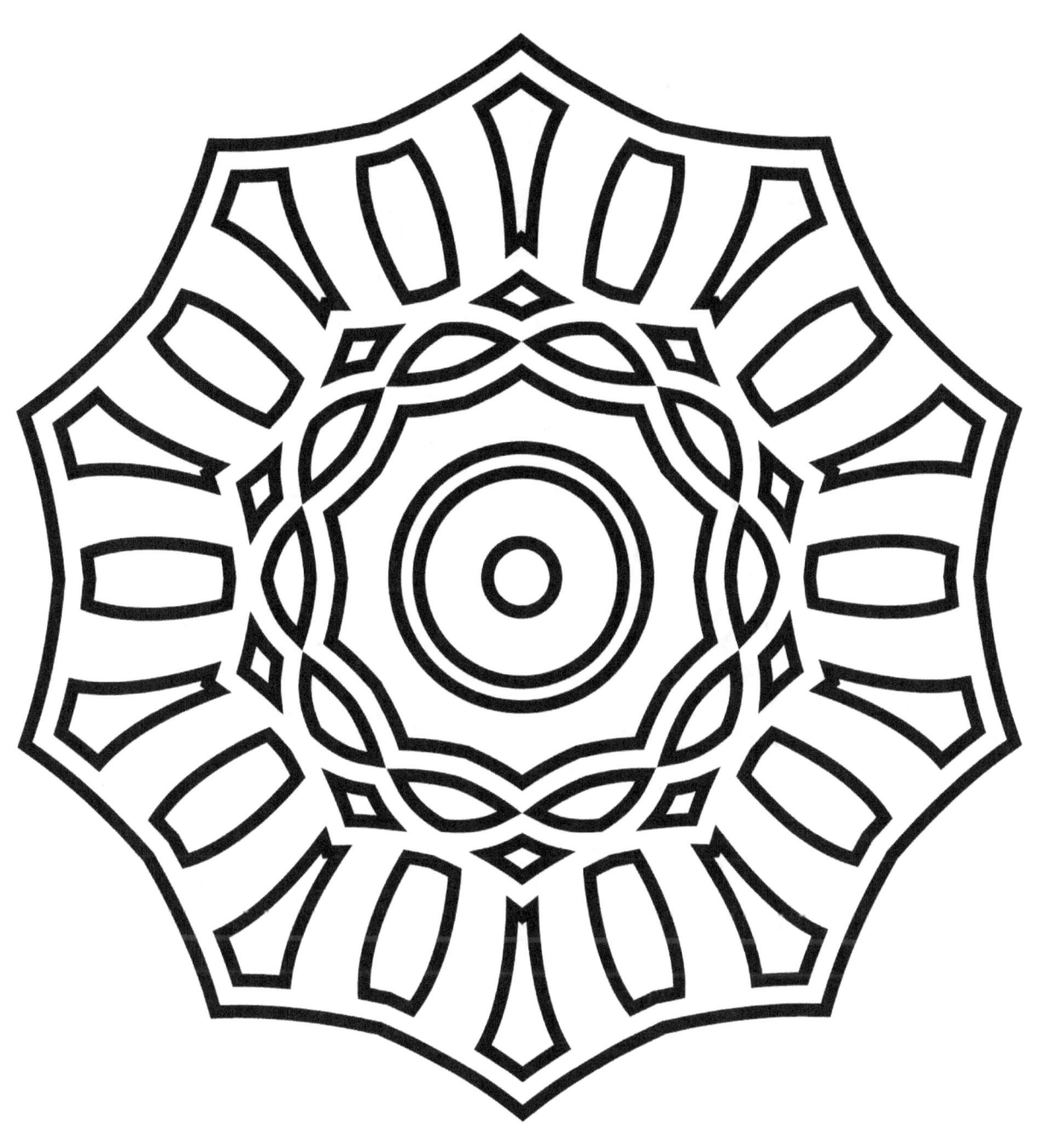

When you reach the top keep climbing

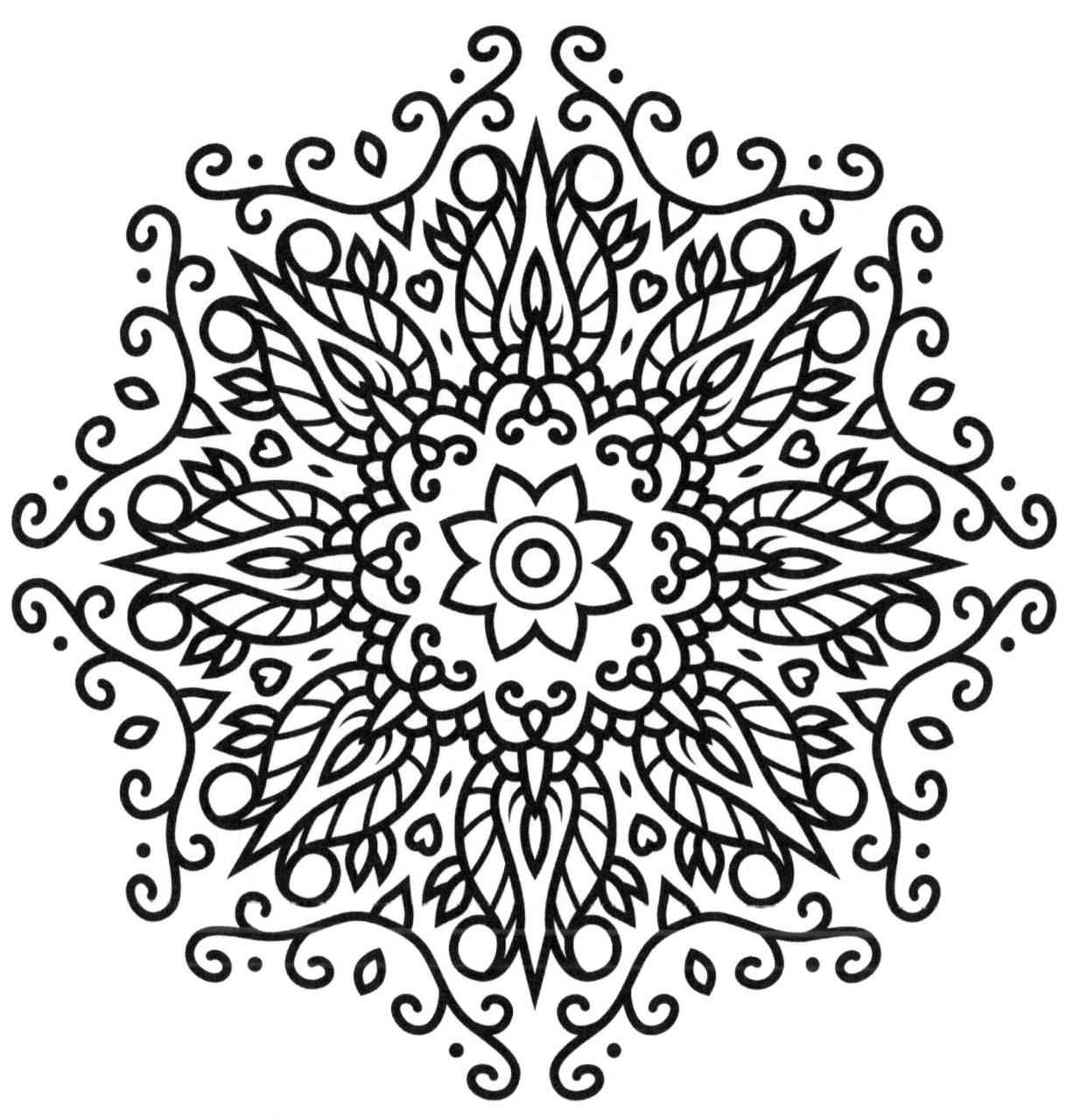

Rule your mind or it will rule you

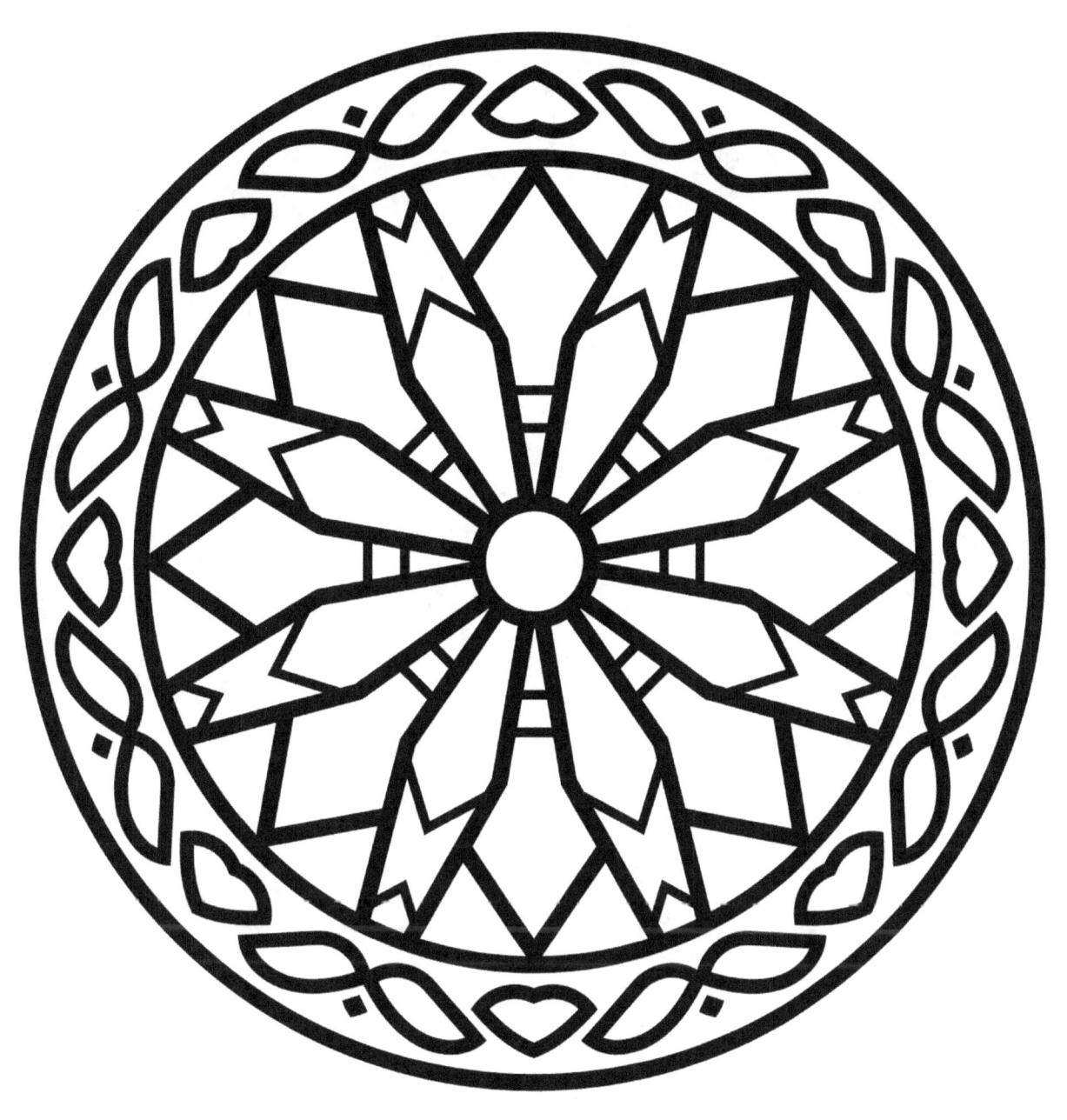

Change how you see and see how you change

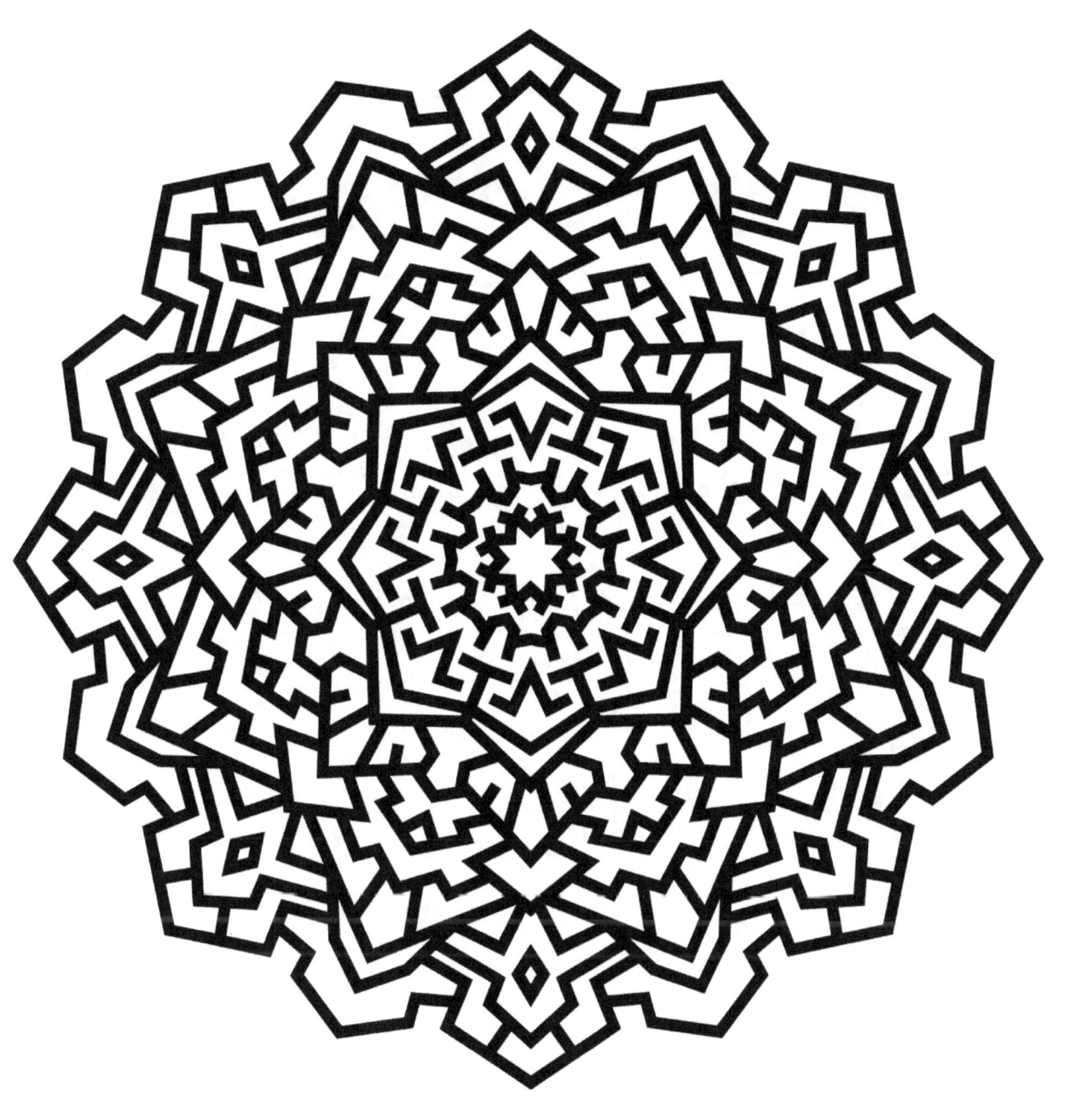

He who envies others does not obtain peace of mind

You must learn a new way to think before you can master a new way to be

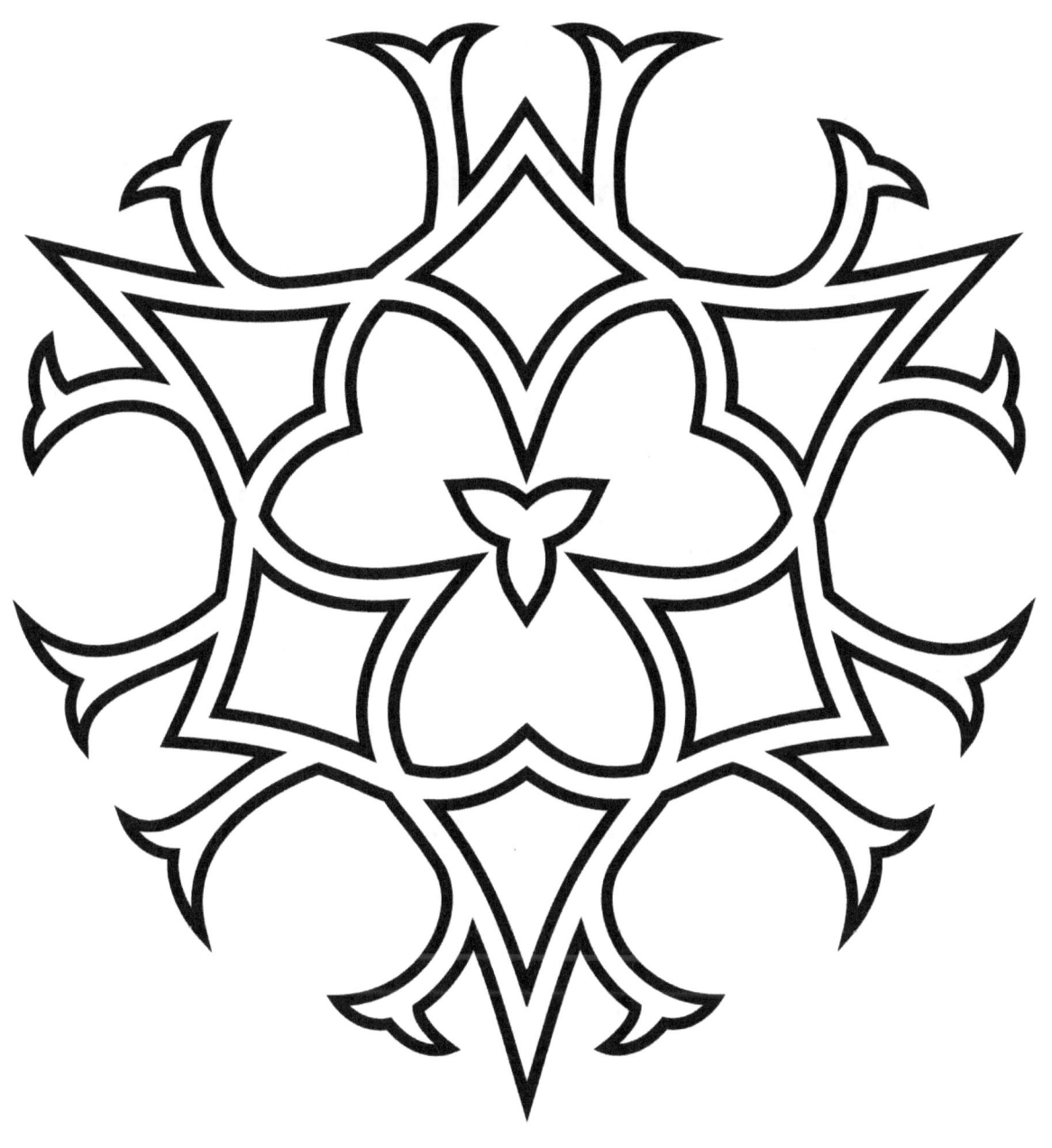

Breathe…it is just a bad day, not a bad life

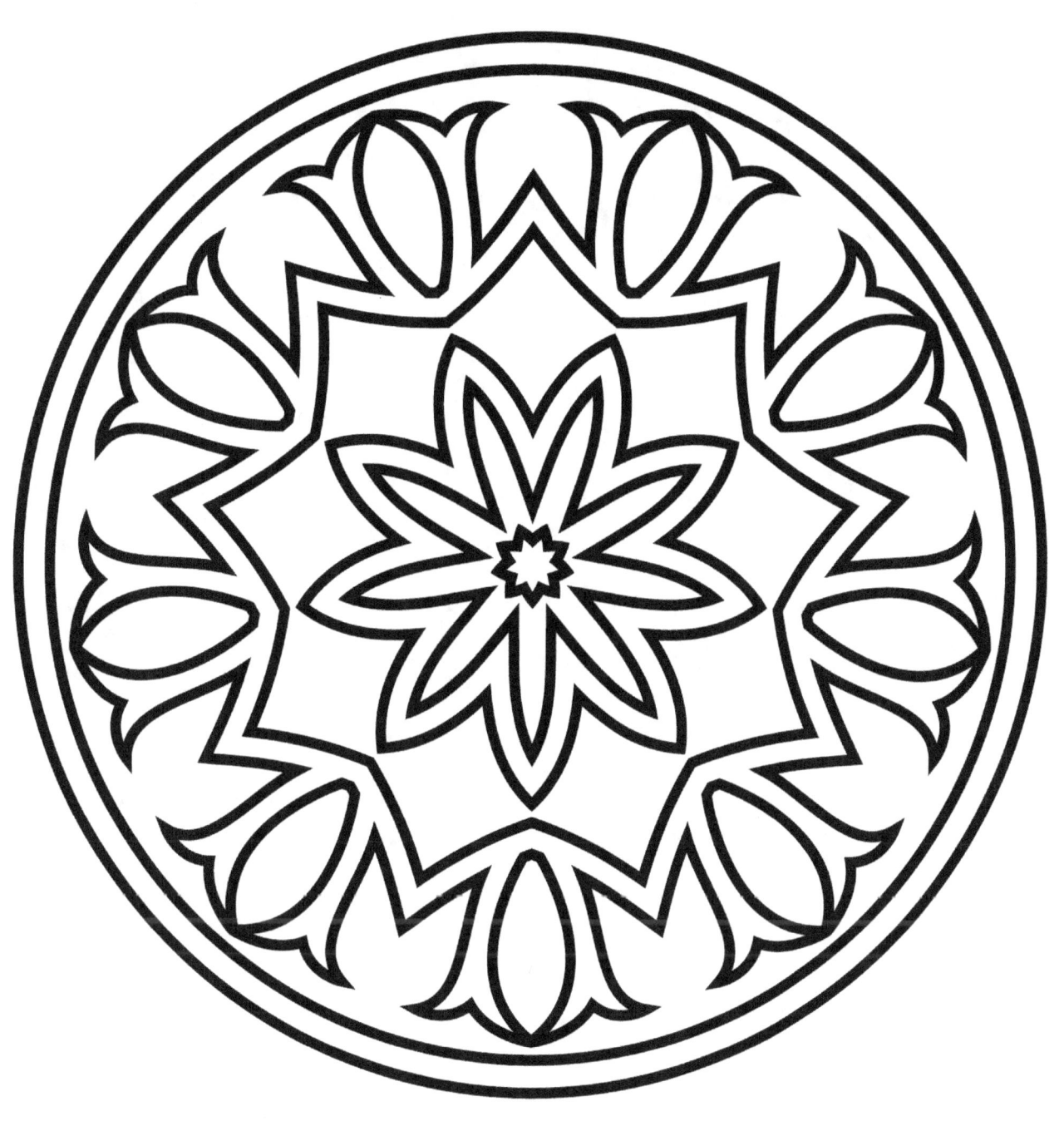

Worrying does not take away tomorrow's troubles...it takes away today's peace

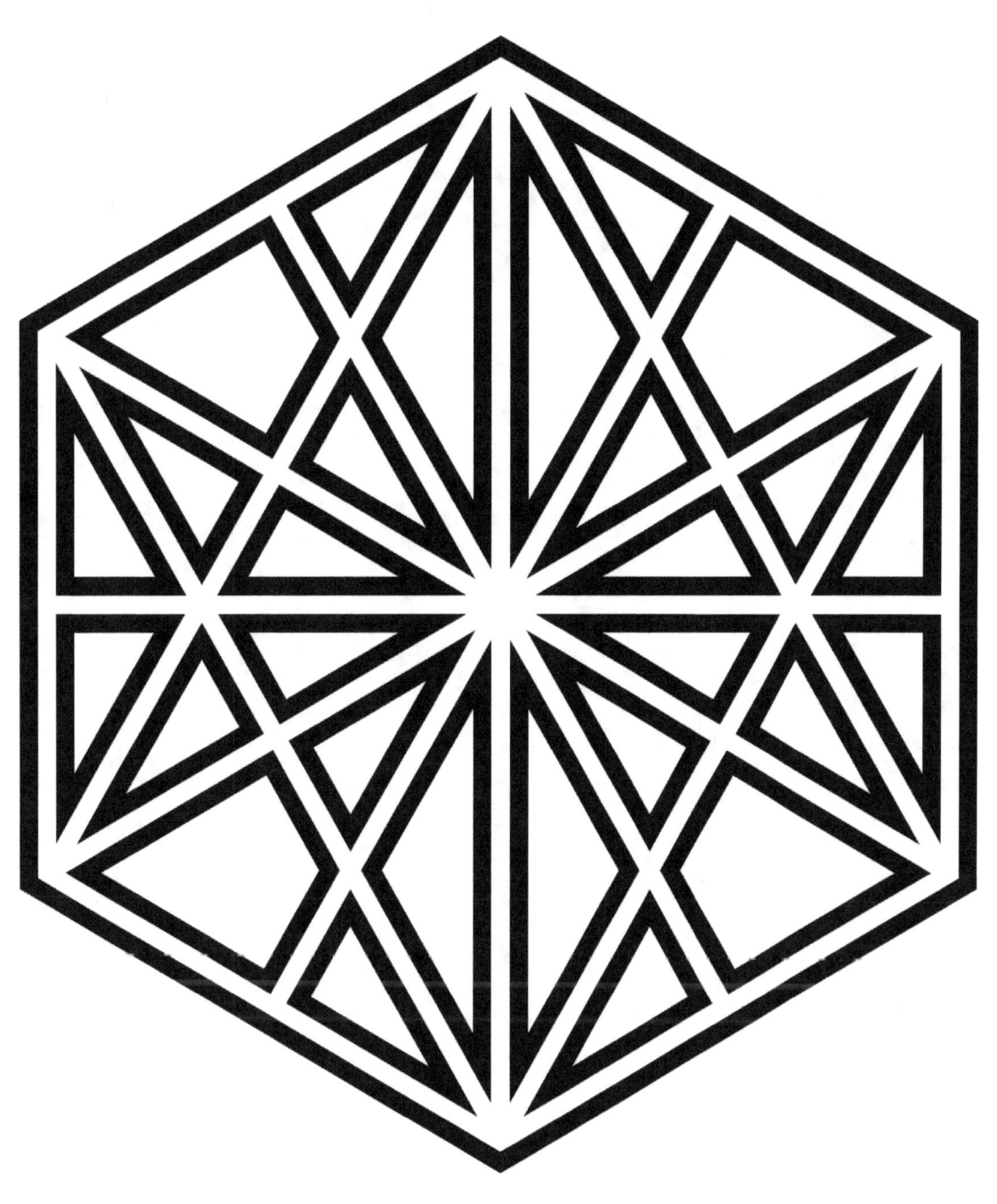

Confidence is silent...insecurities are loud

Every bad thing has a good side

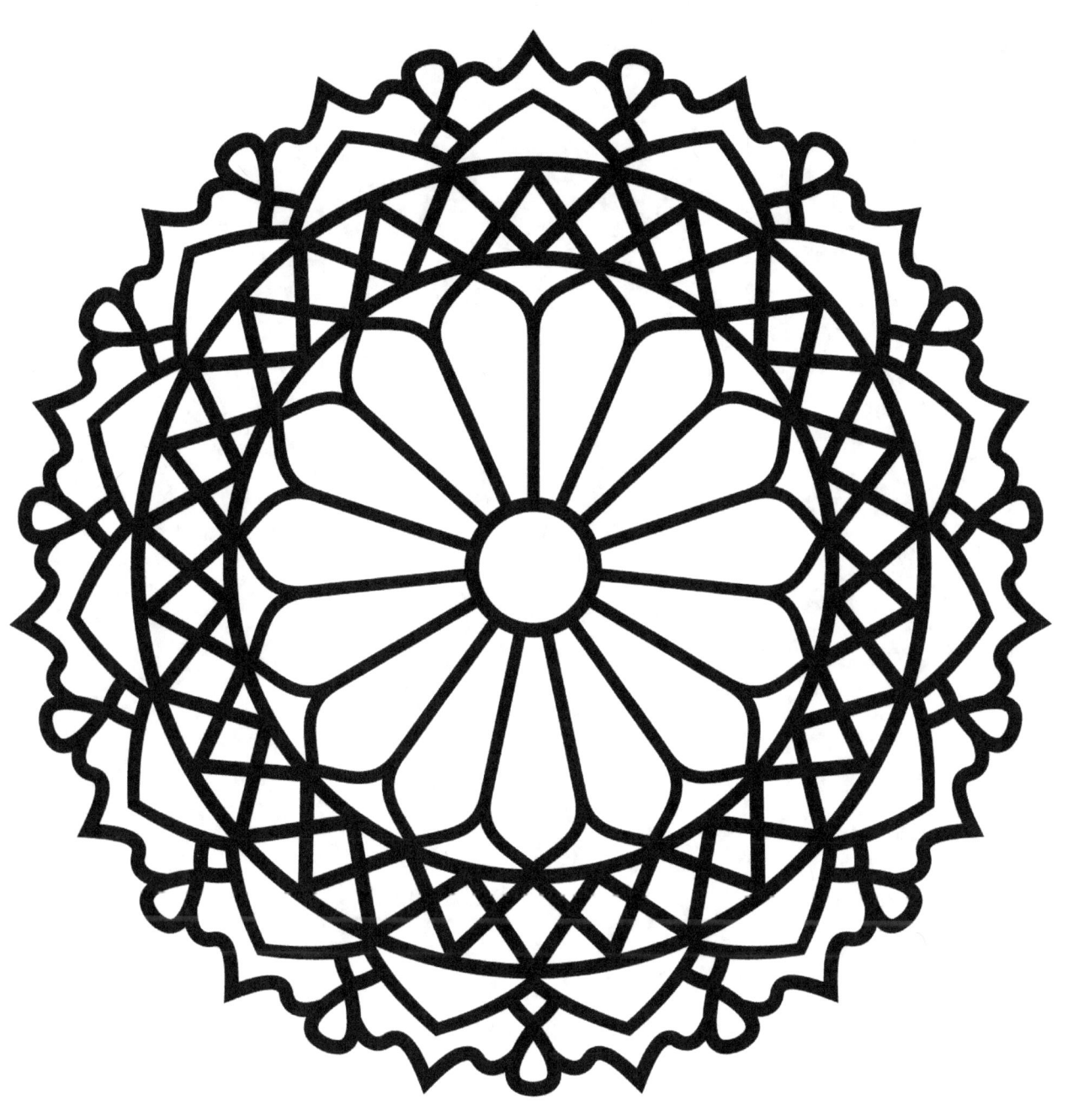

Do less with more focus

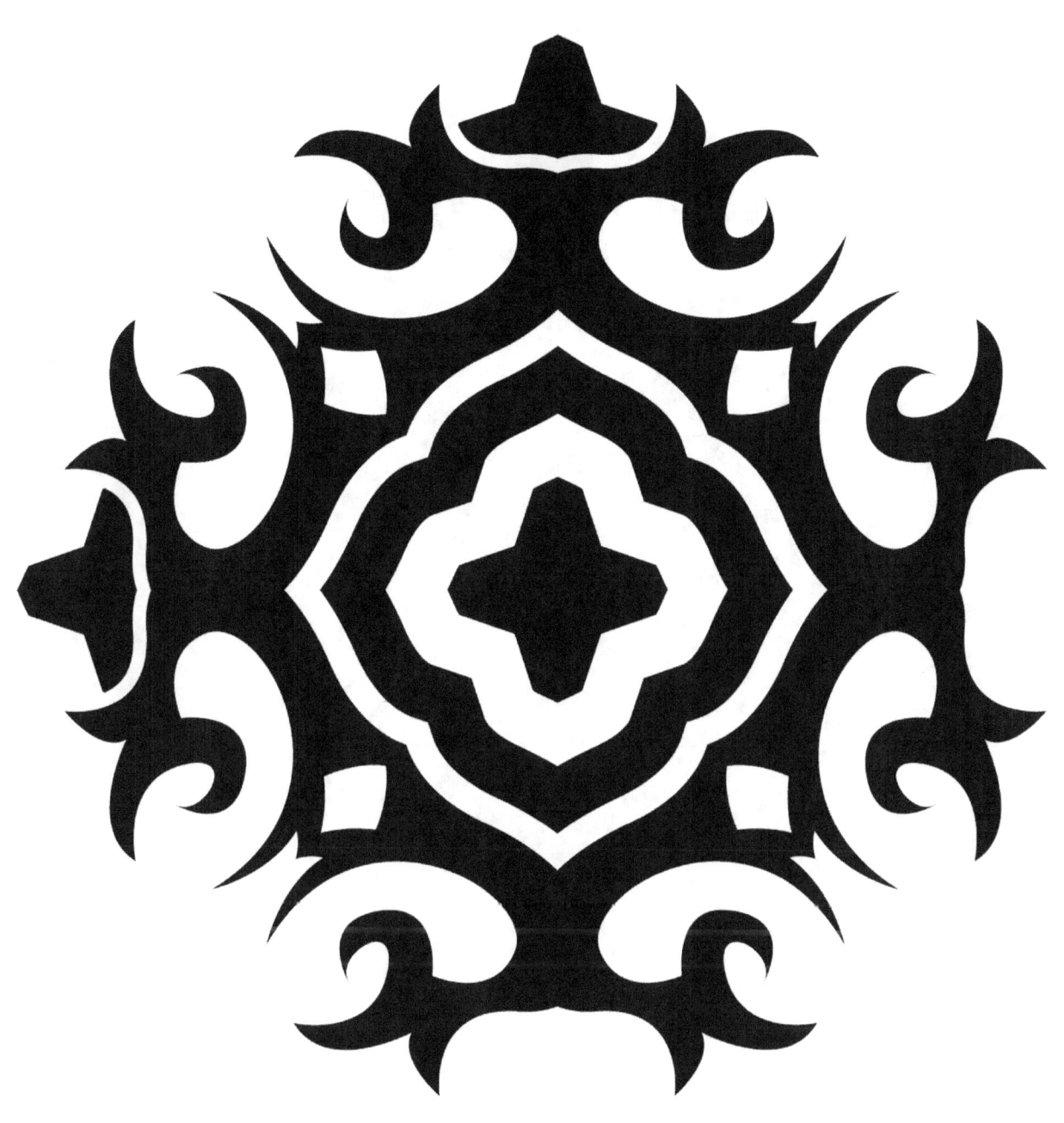

Be someone you want to be around

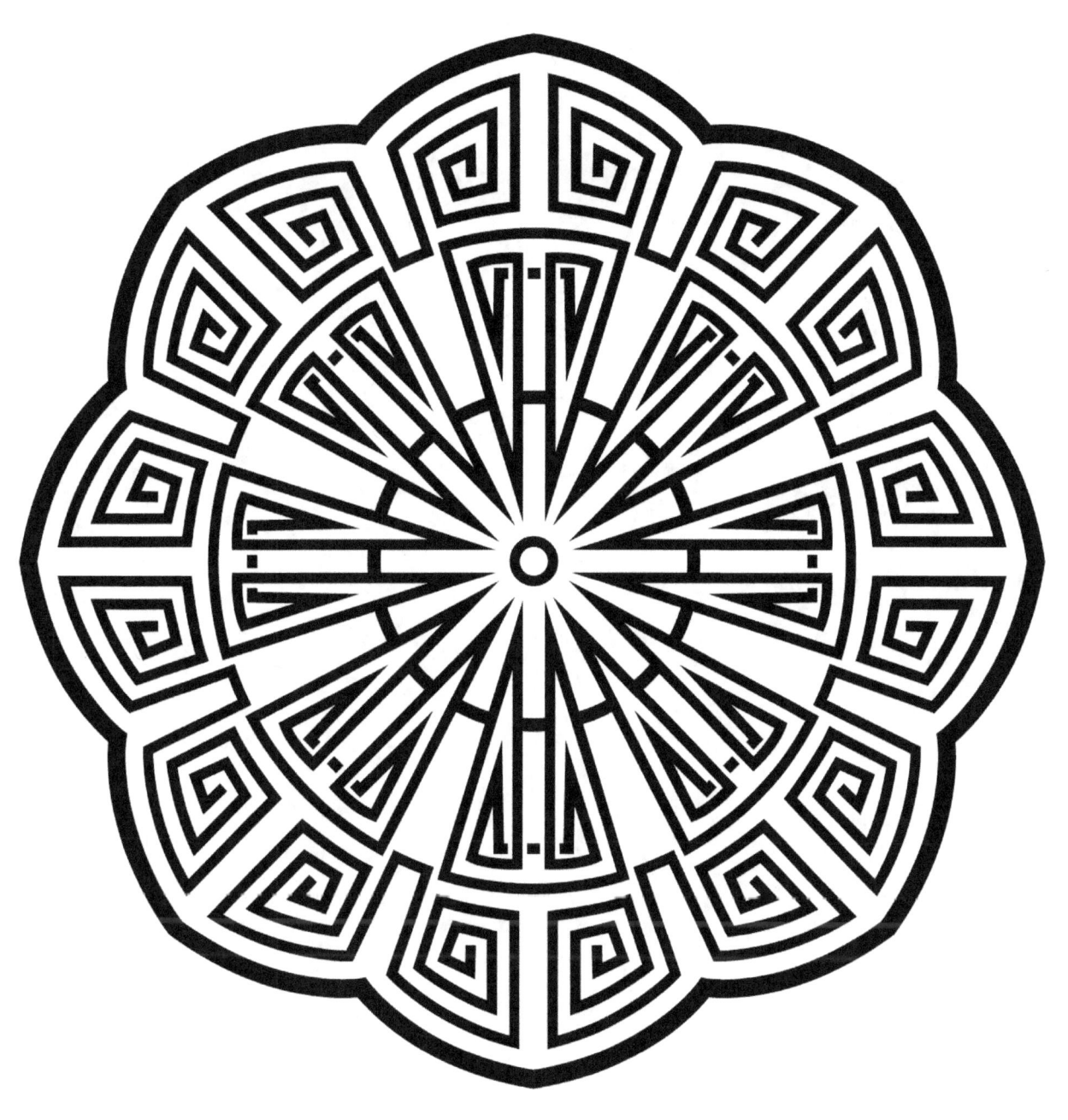

Silence is a source of great strength

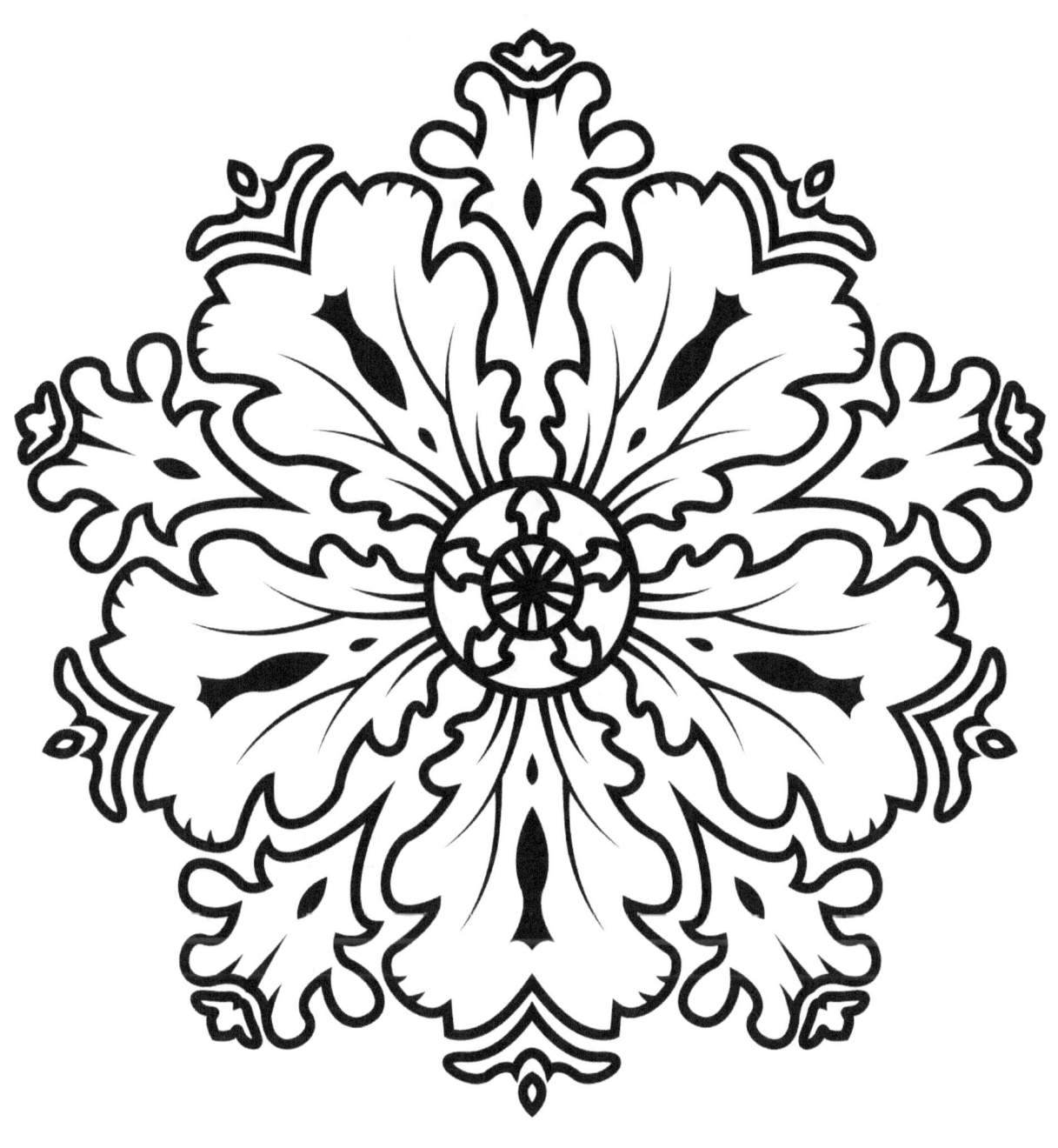

If you truly loved yourself you could never hurt another

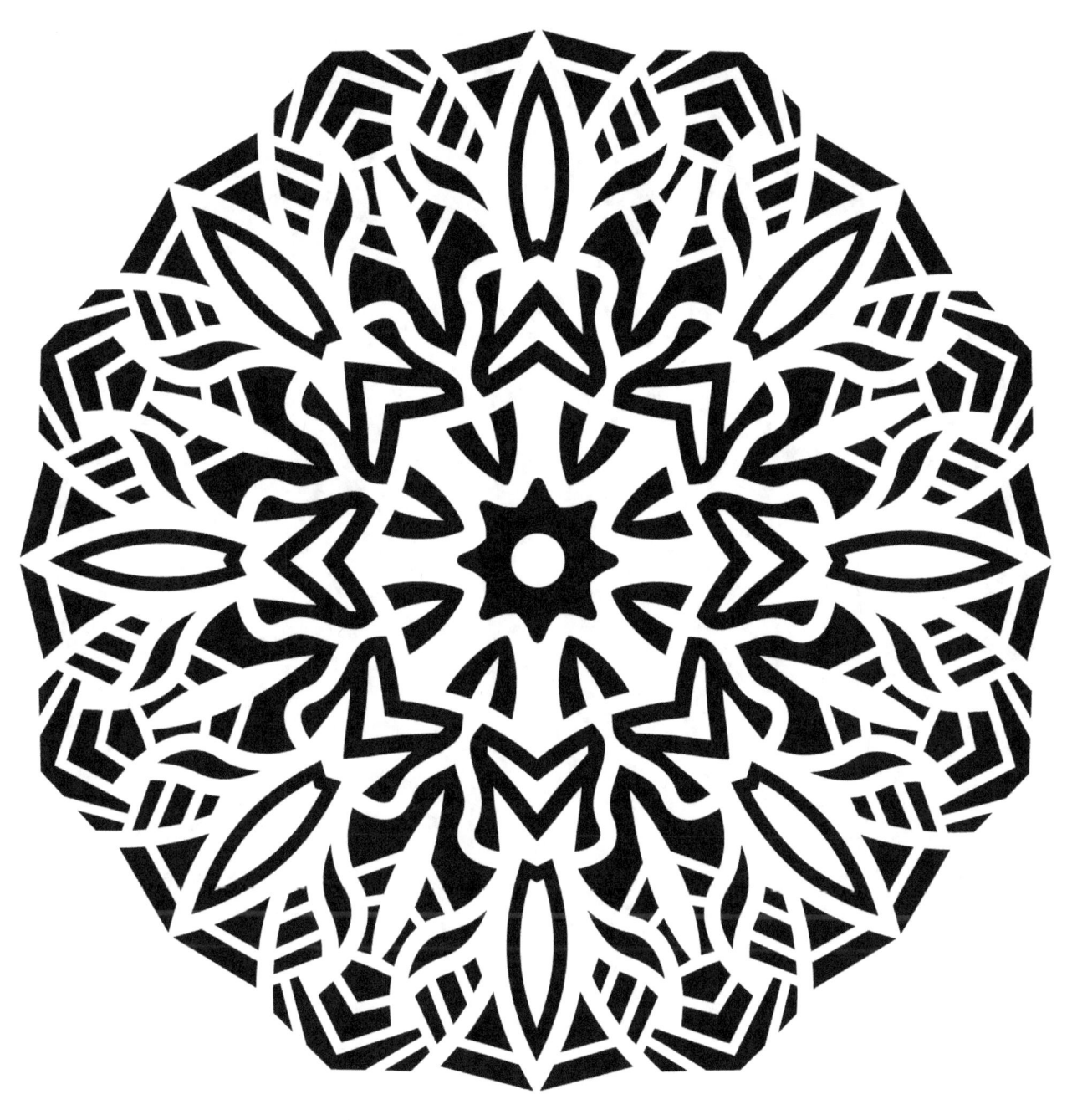

Act without expectations

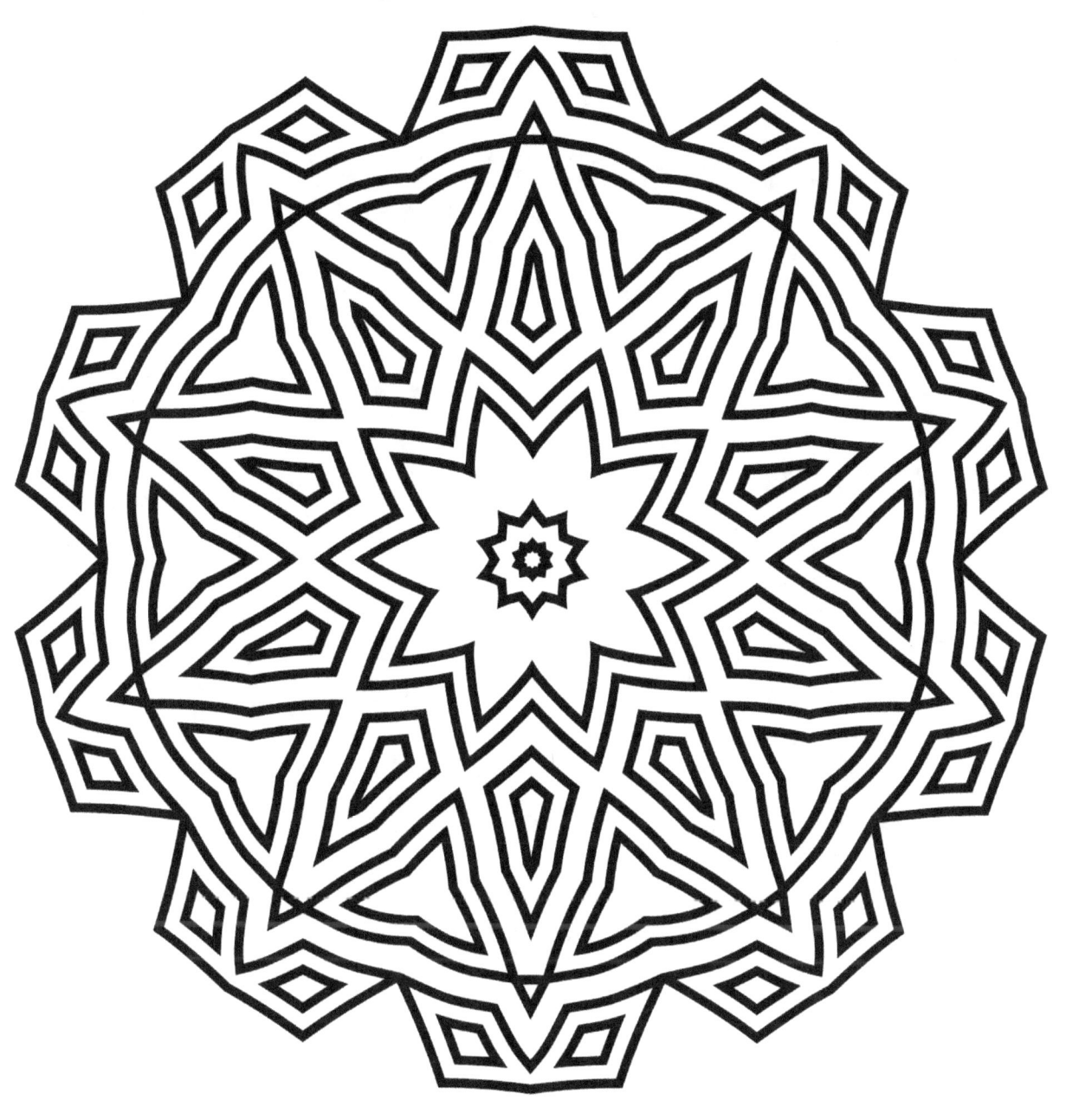

To be truly ignorant, be content with your own knowledge

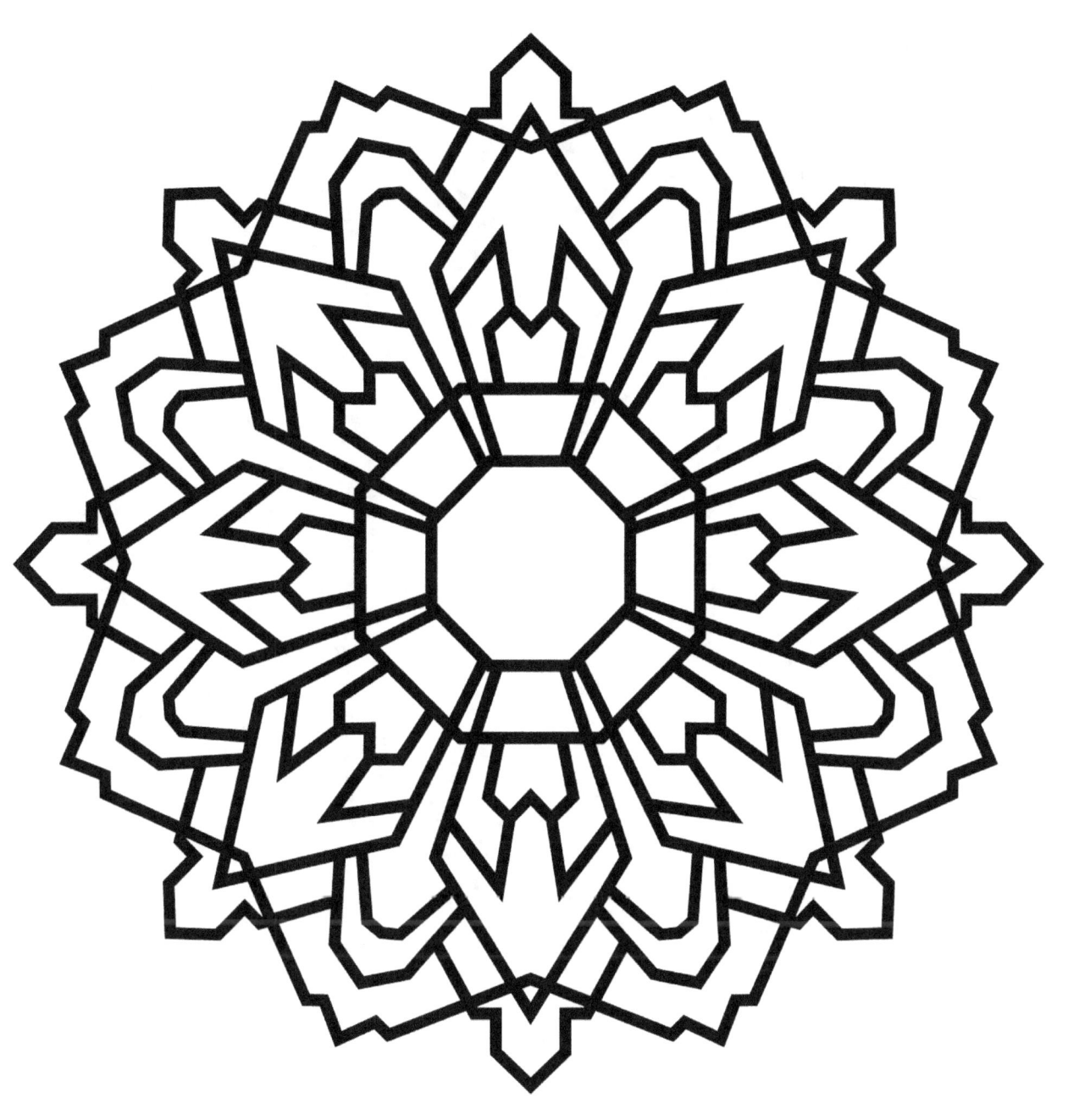

What we do in life echoes in eternity

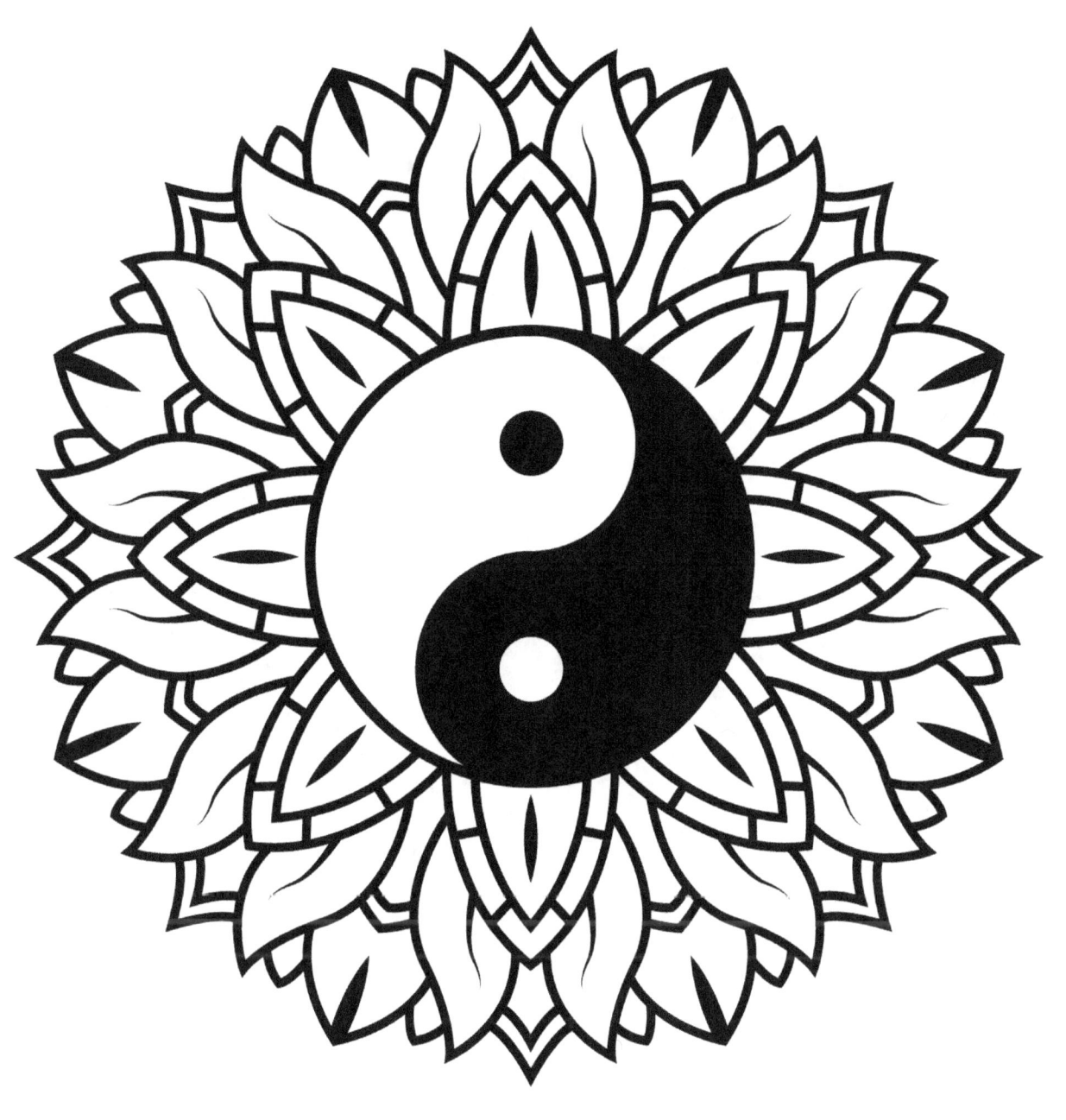

This moment is full of wonders

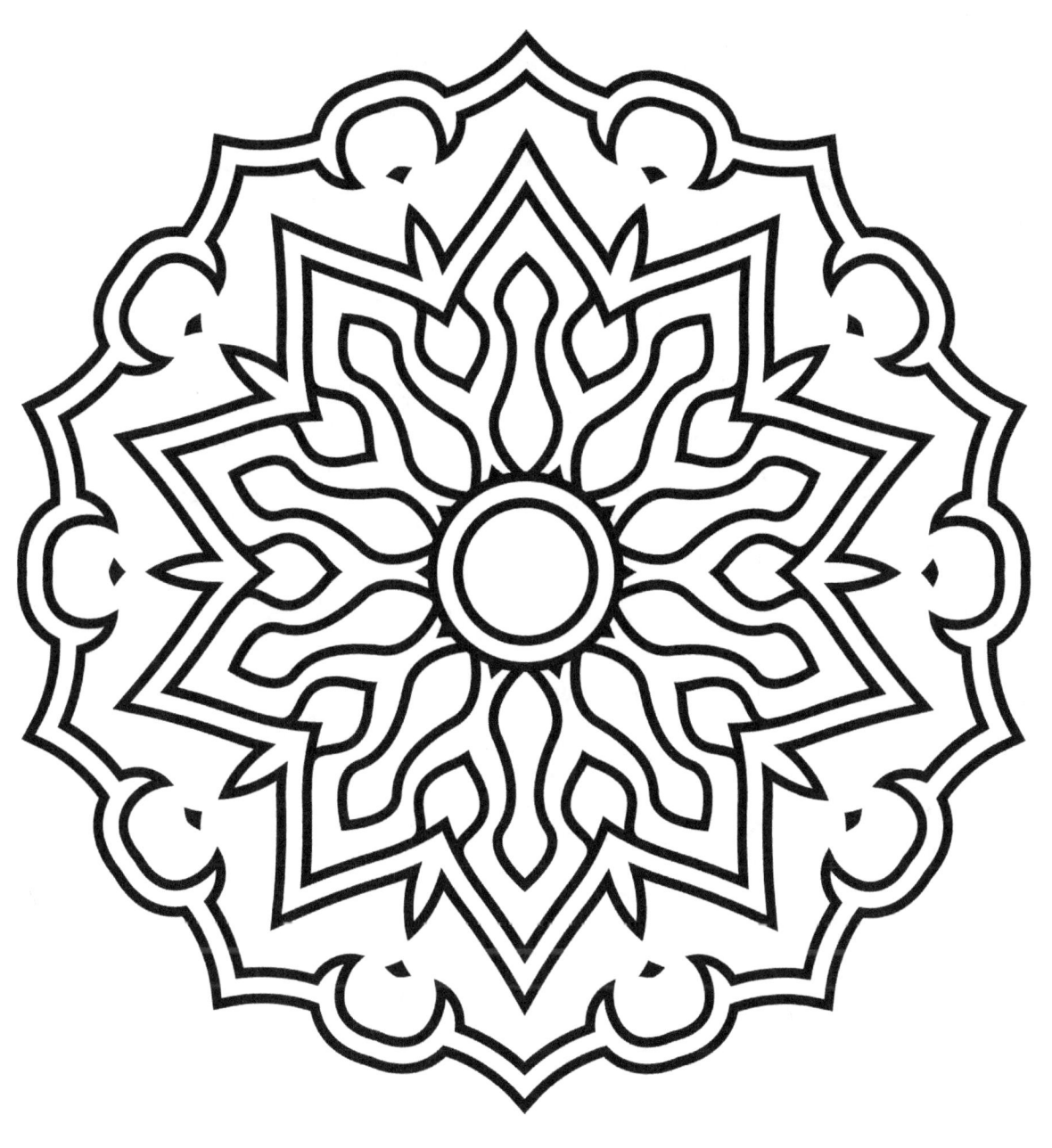

Happiness is a journey, not a destination

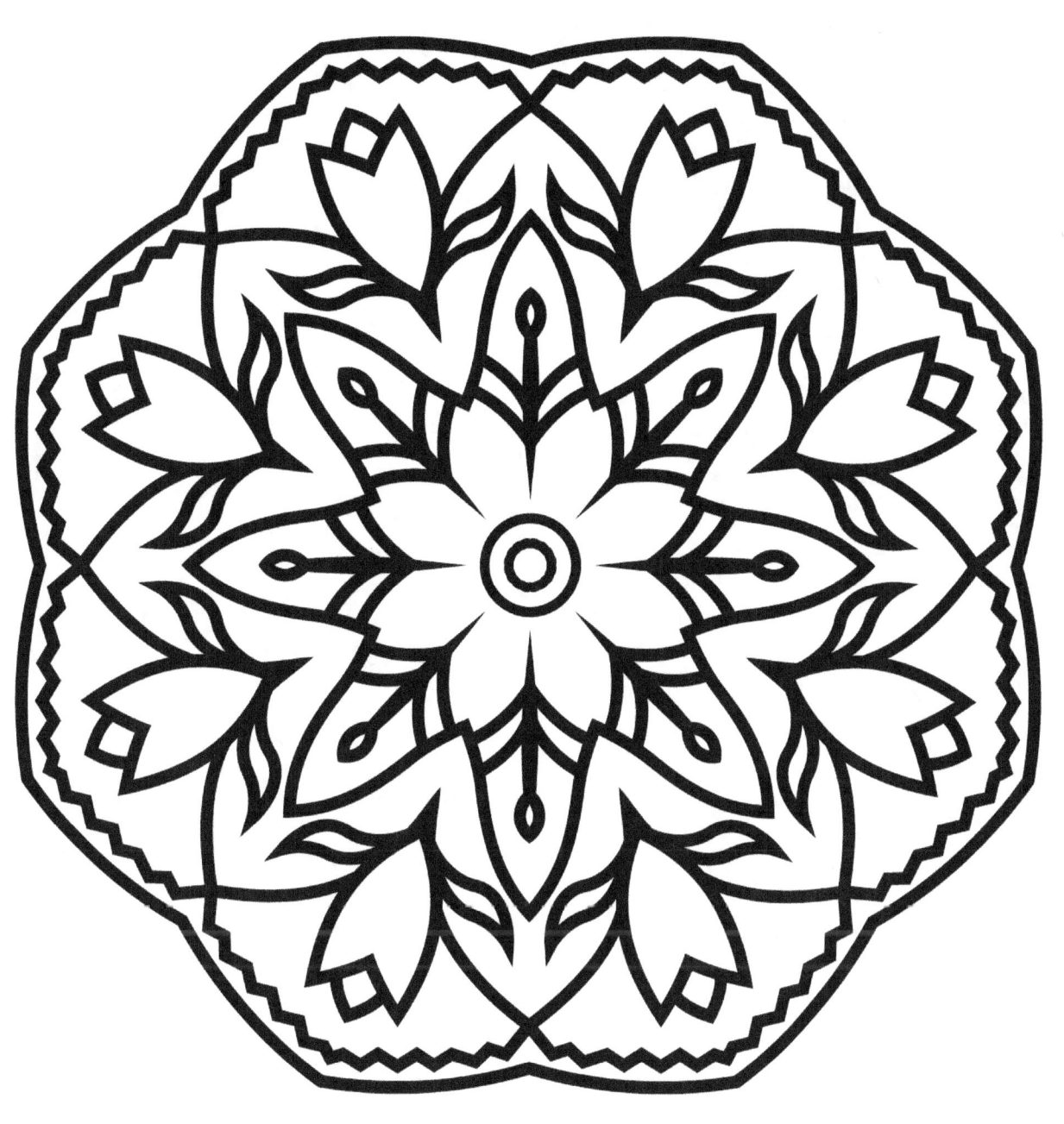

Positivity breeds prosperity

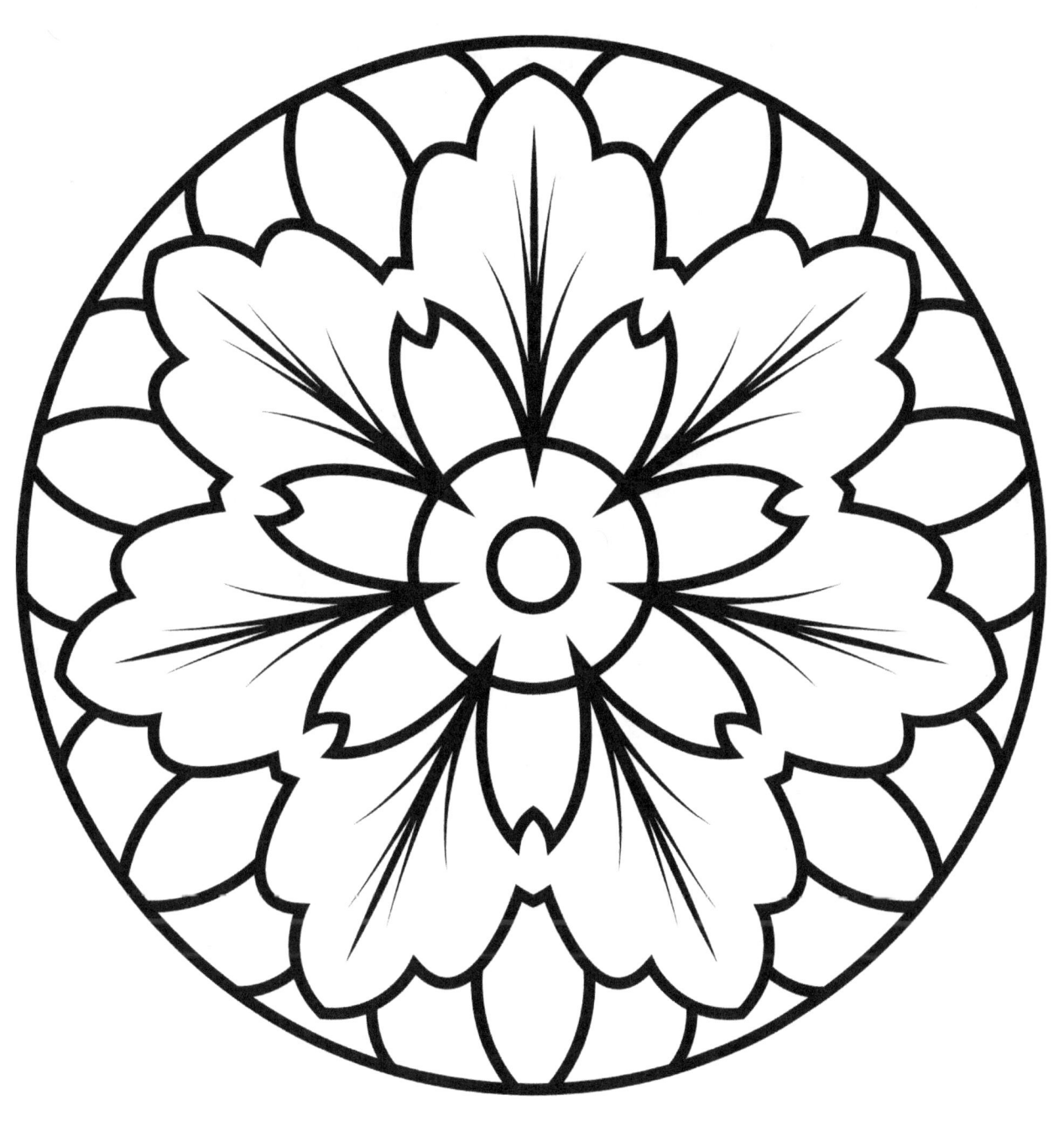

Listen to your body, it is smarter than you are

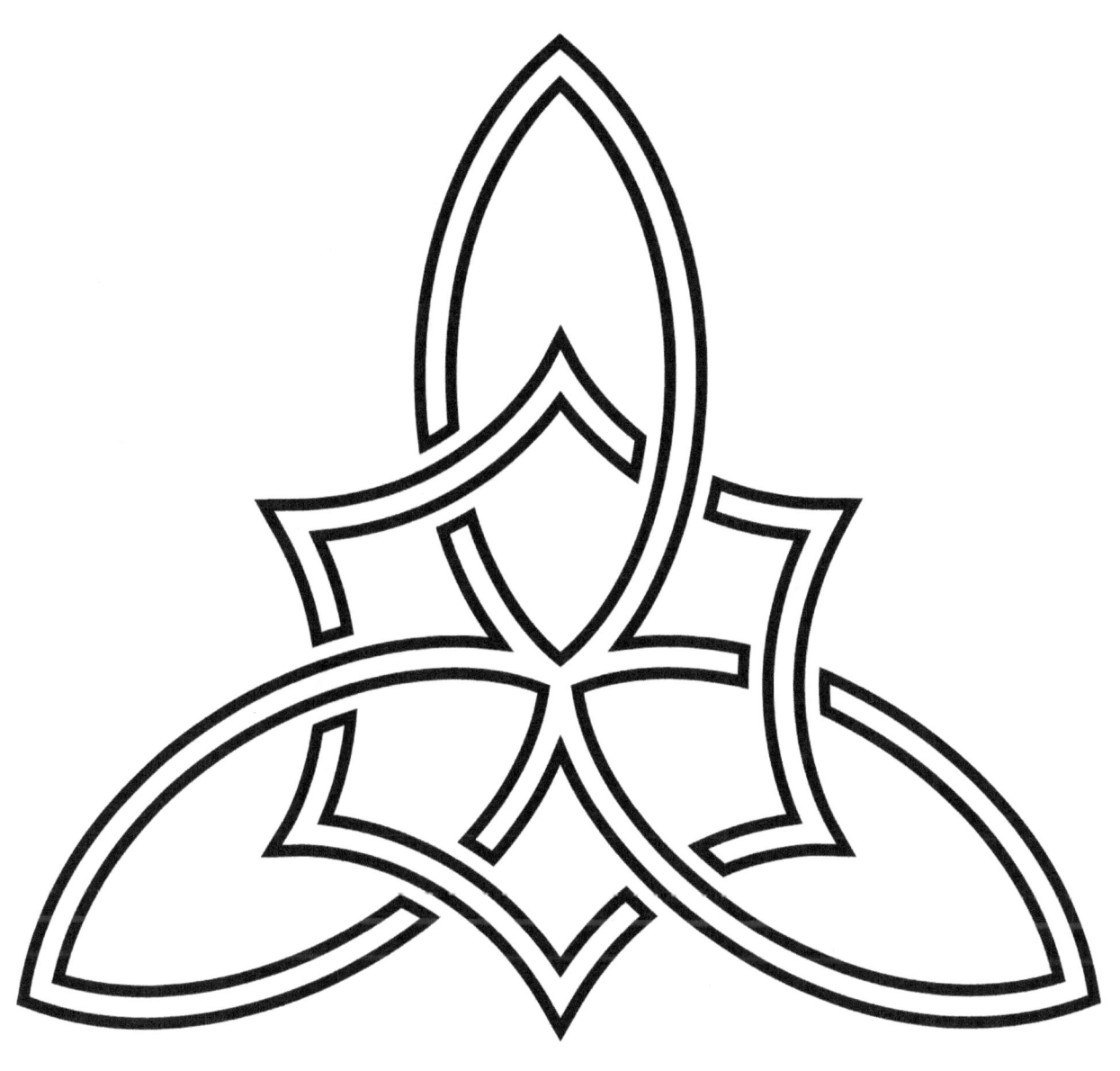

Do what they think you can't do

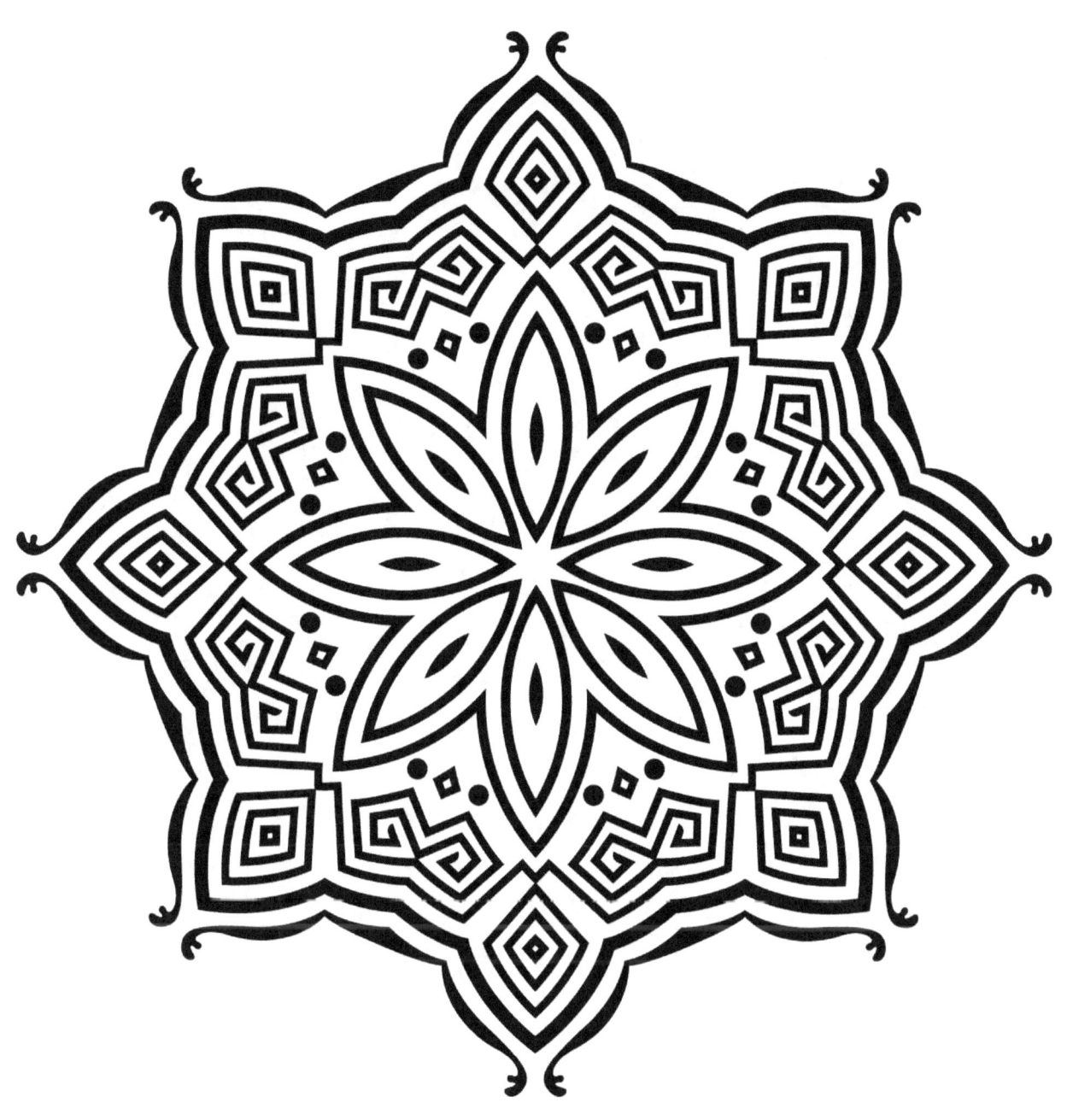

Think happy…stay happy

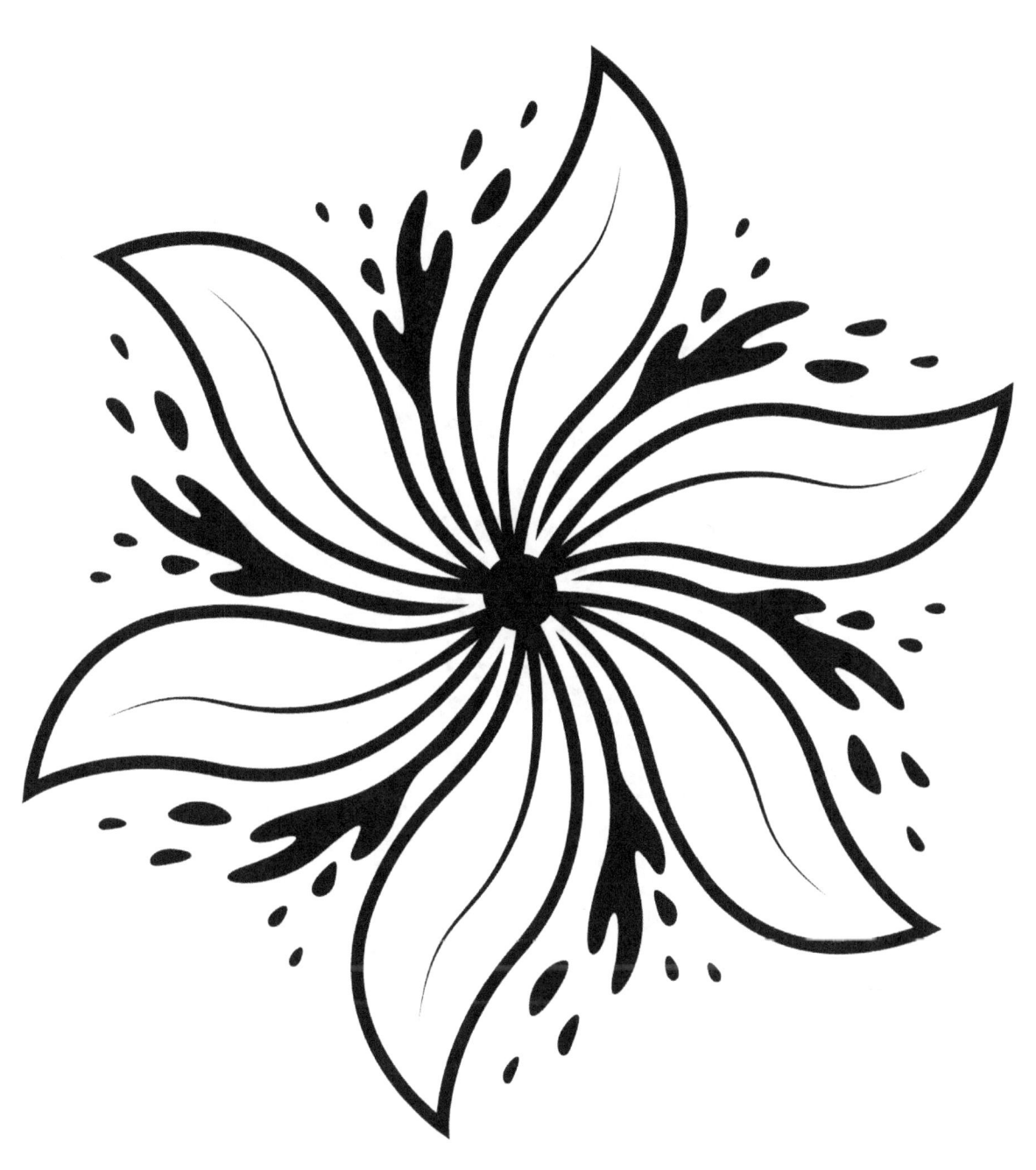

Don't quit your day dream

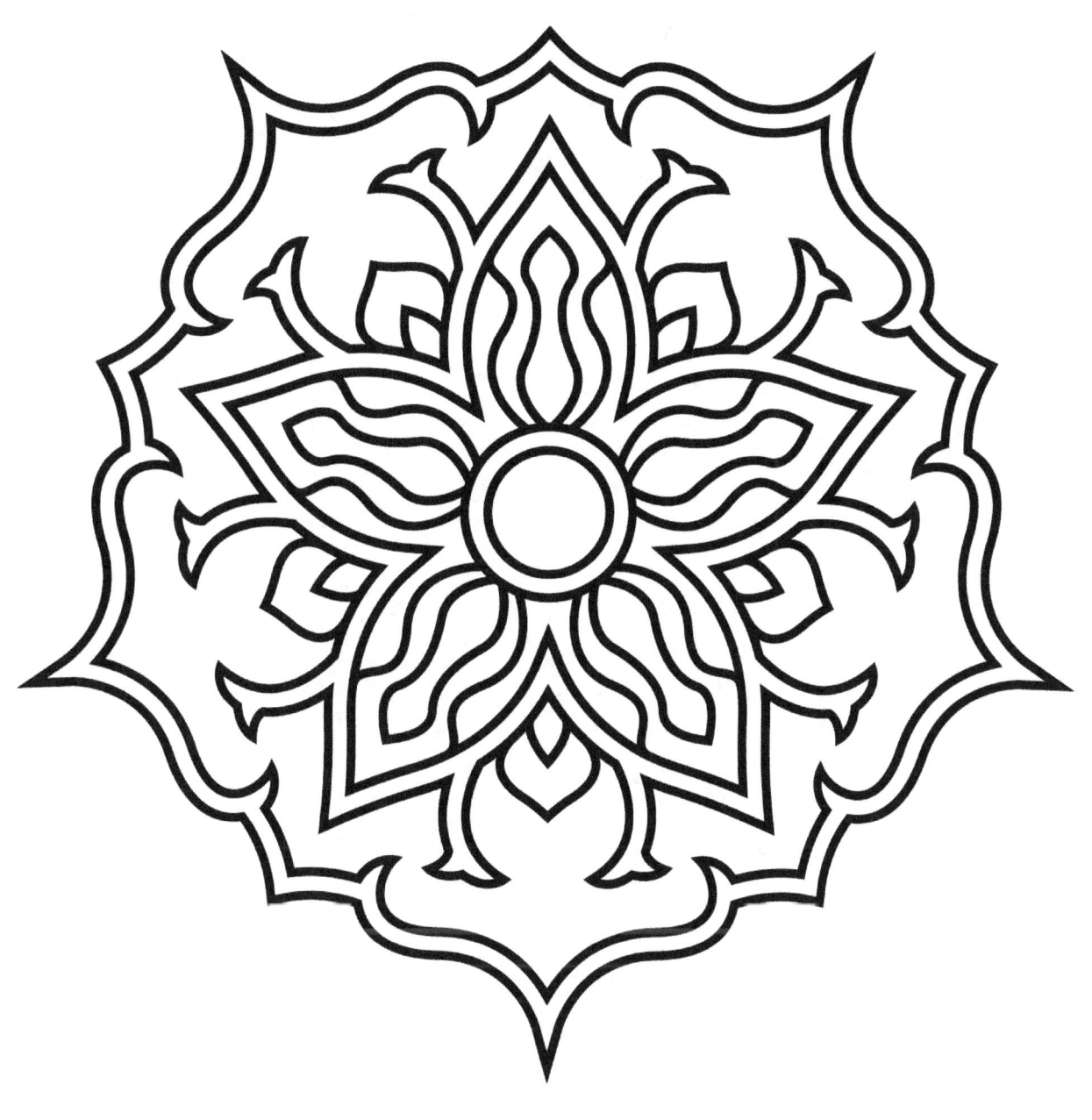

Don't be afraid of being a beginner

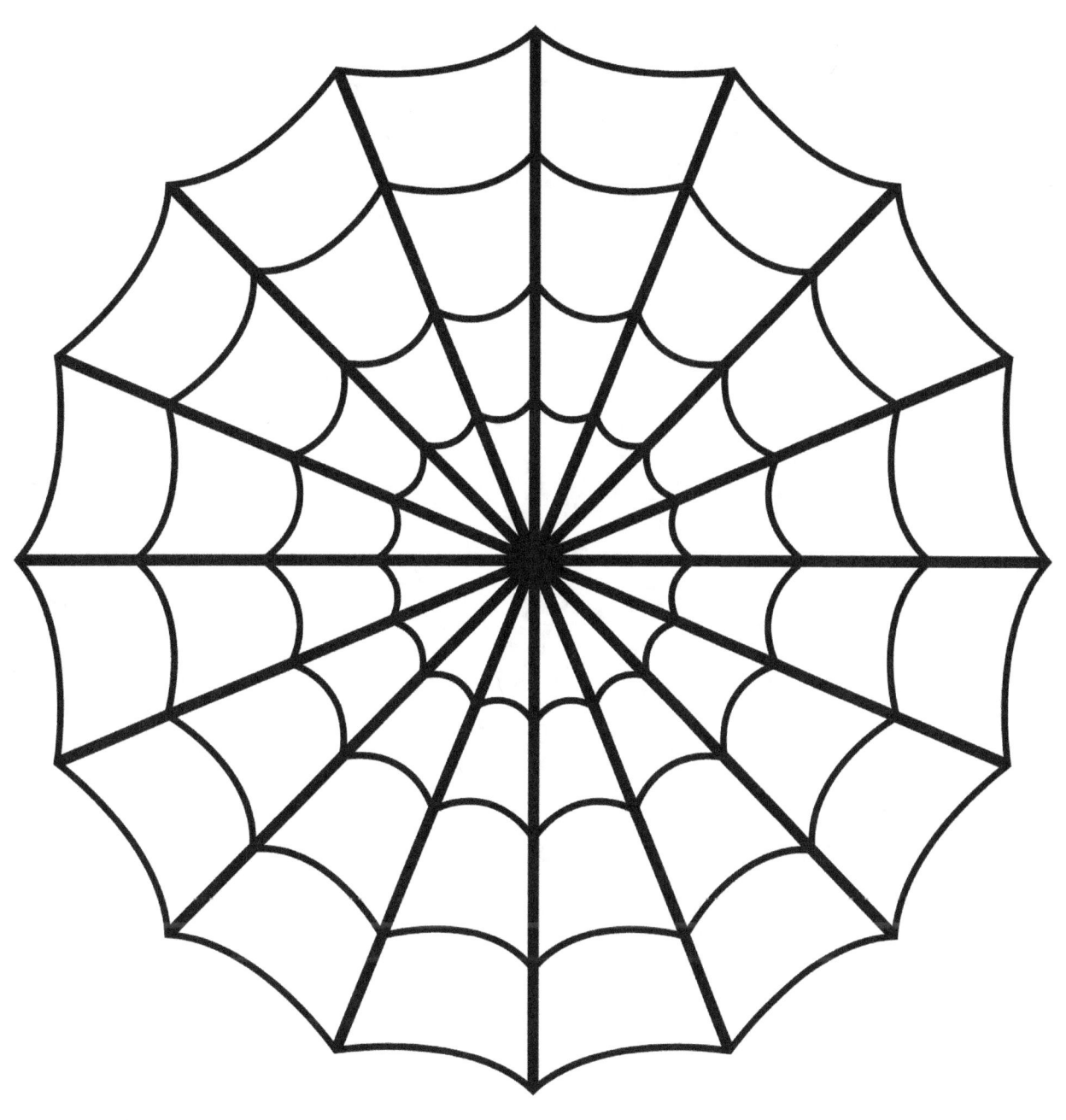

Every success story started with a dream

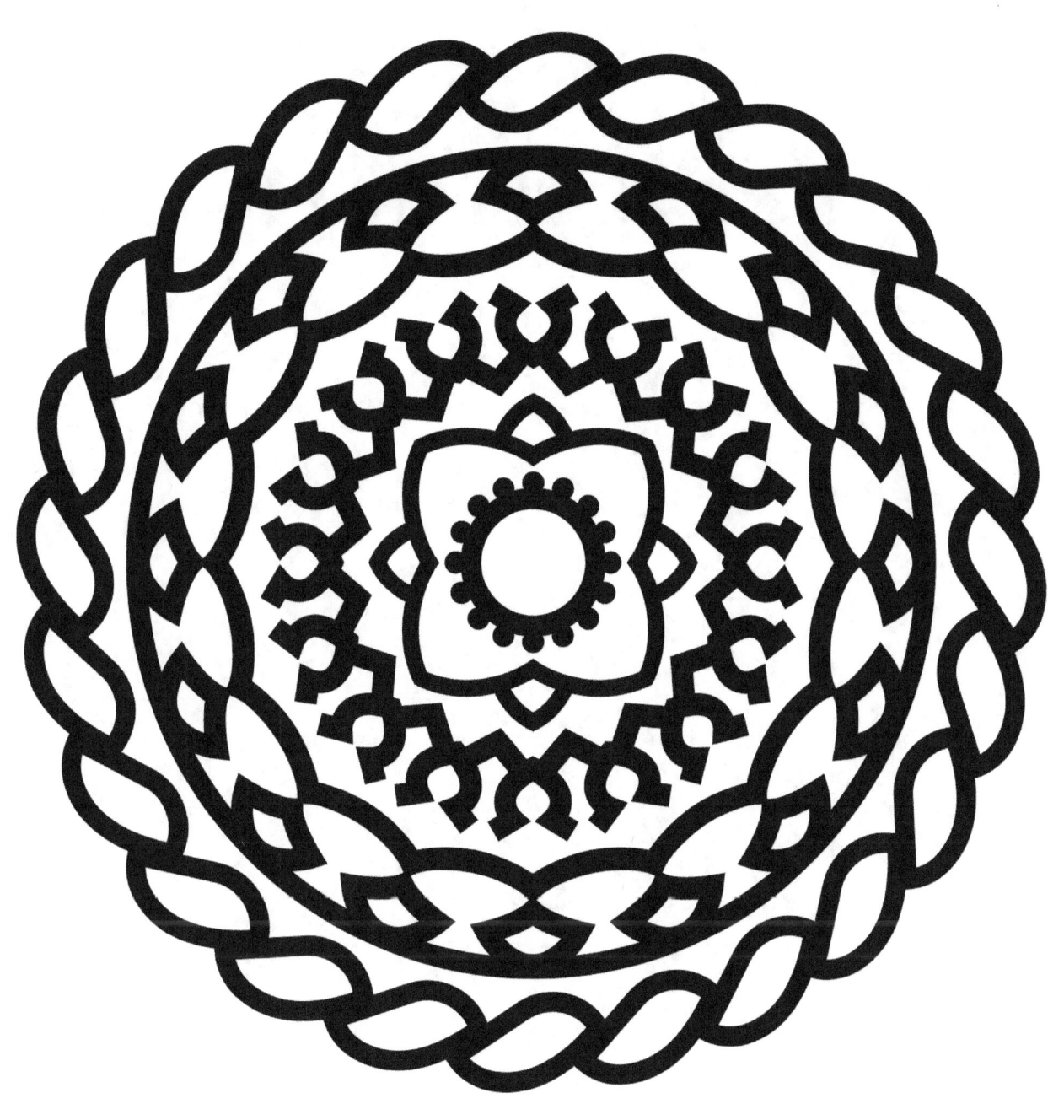

Do not learn how to react…learn how to respond

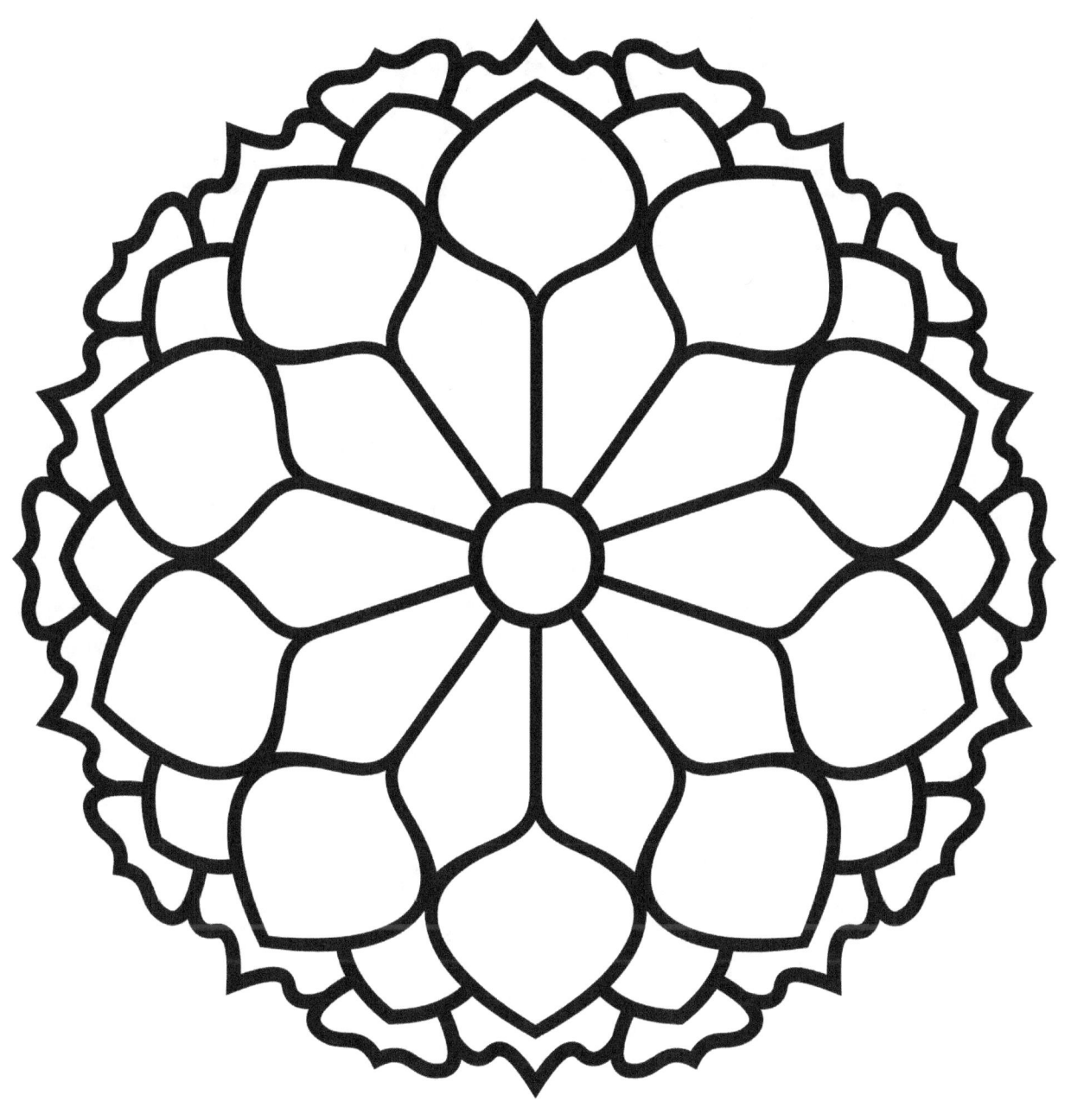

If opportunity doesn't knock…build the door

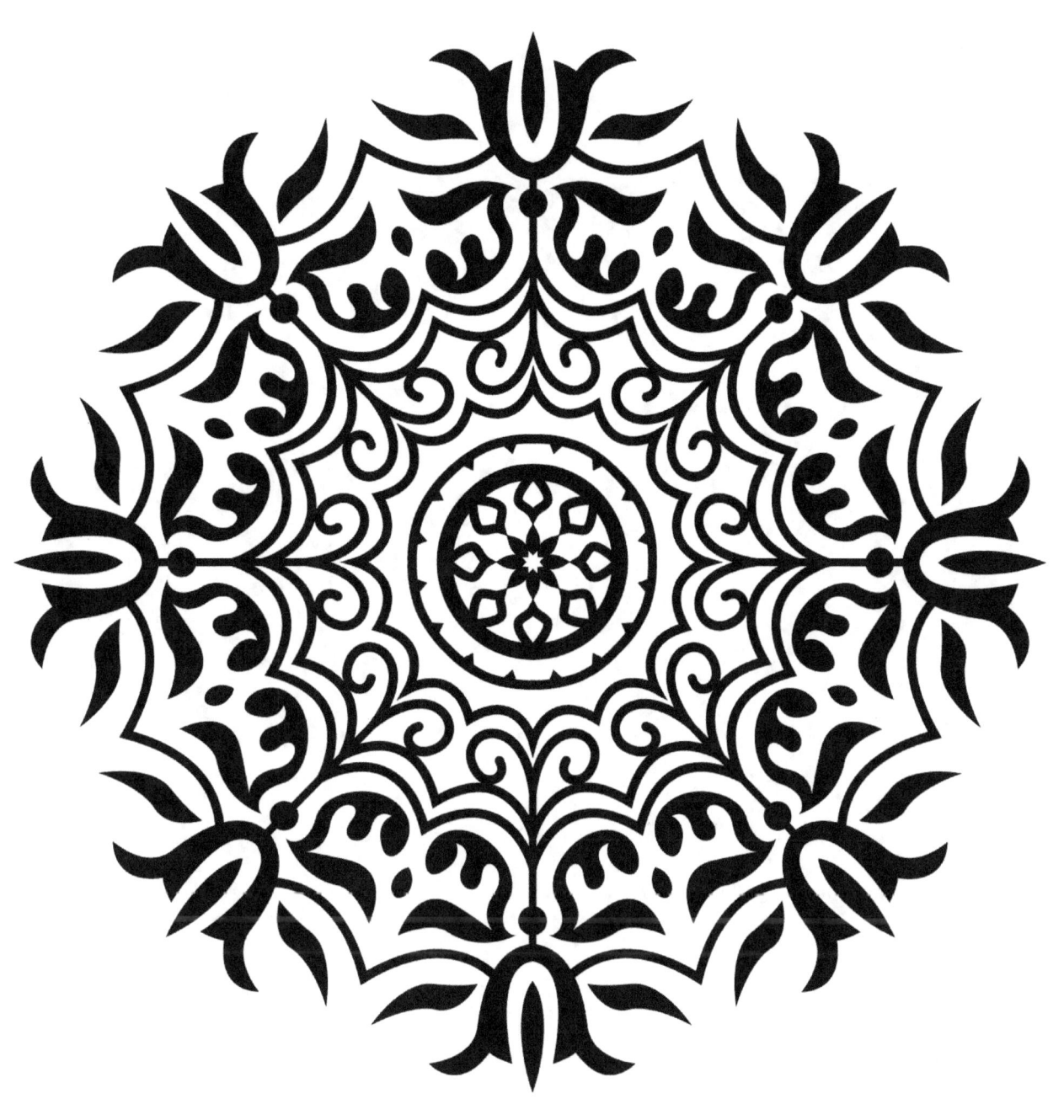

Life is all around us

Start each day with a grateful heart

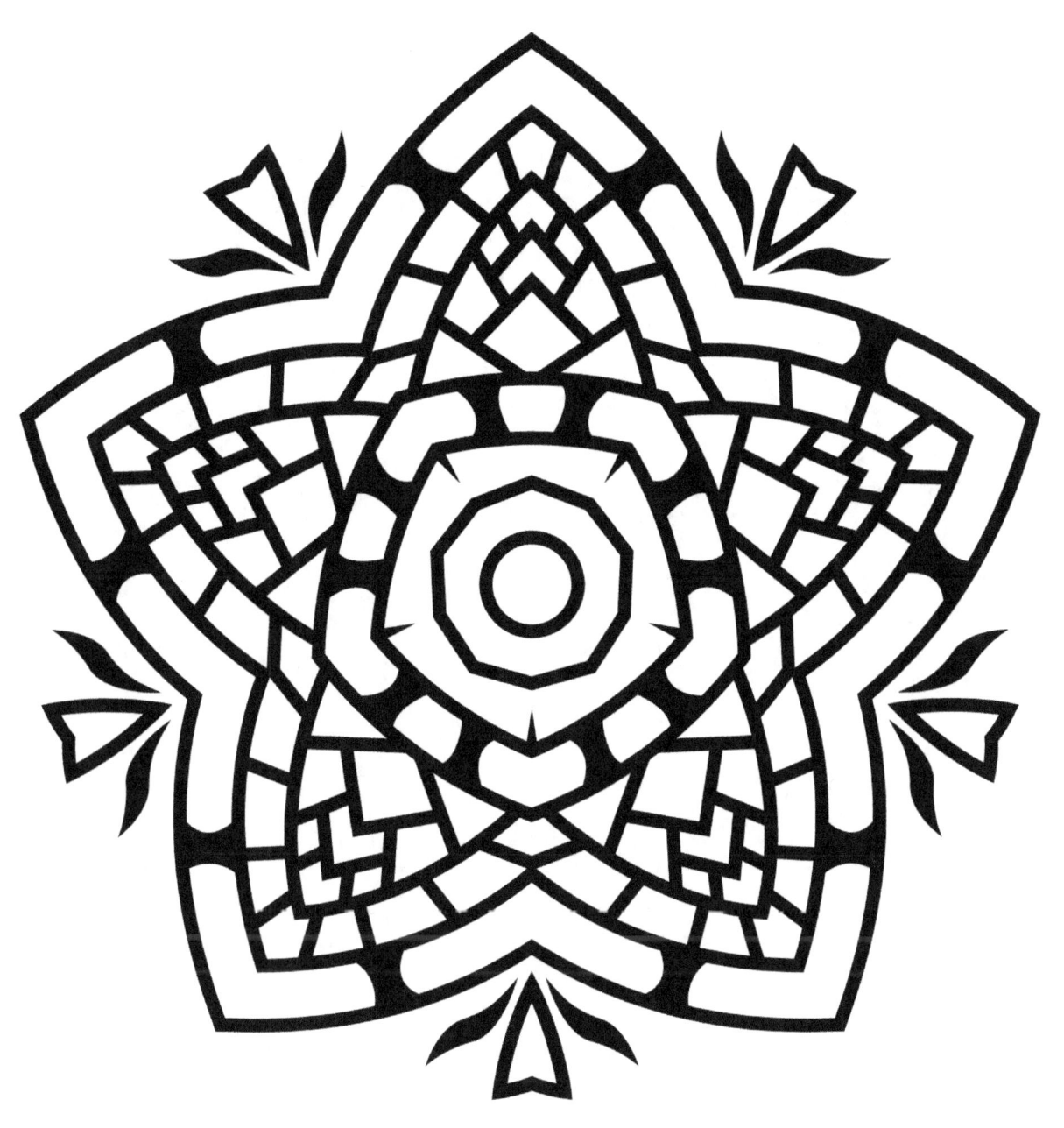

Don't let your motivation burn out

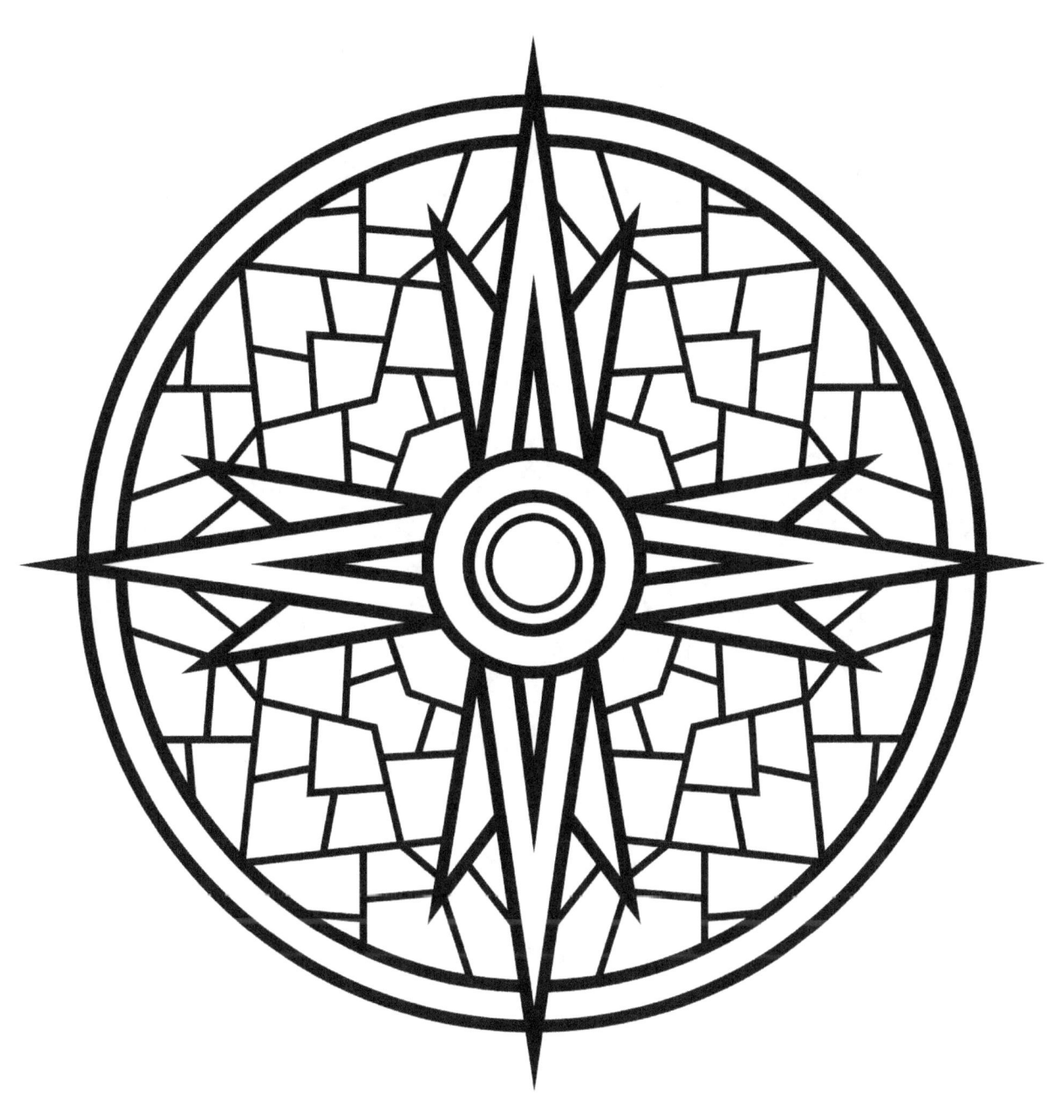

We are here for each other

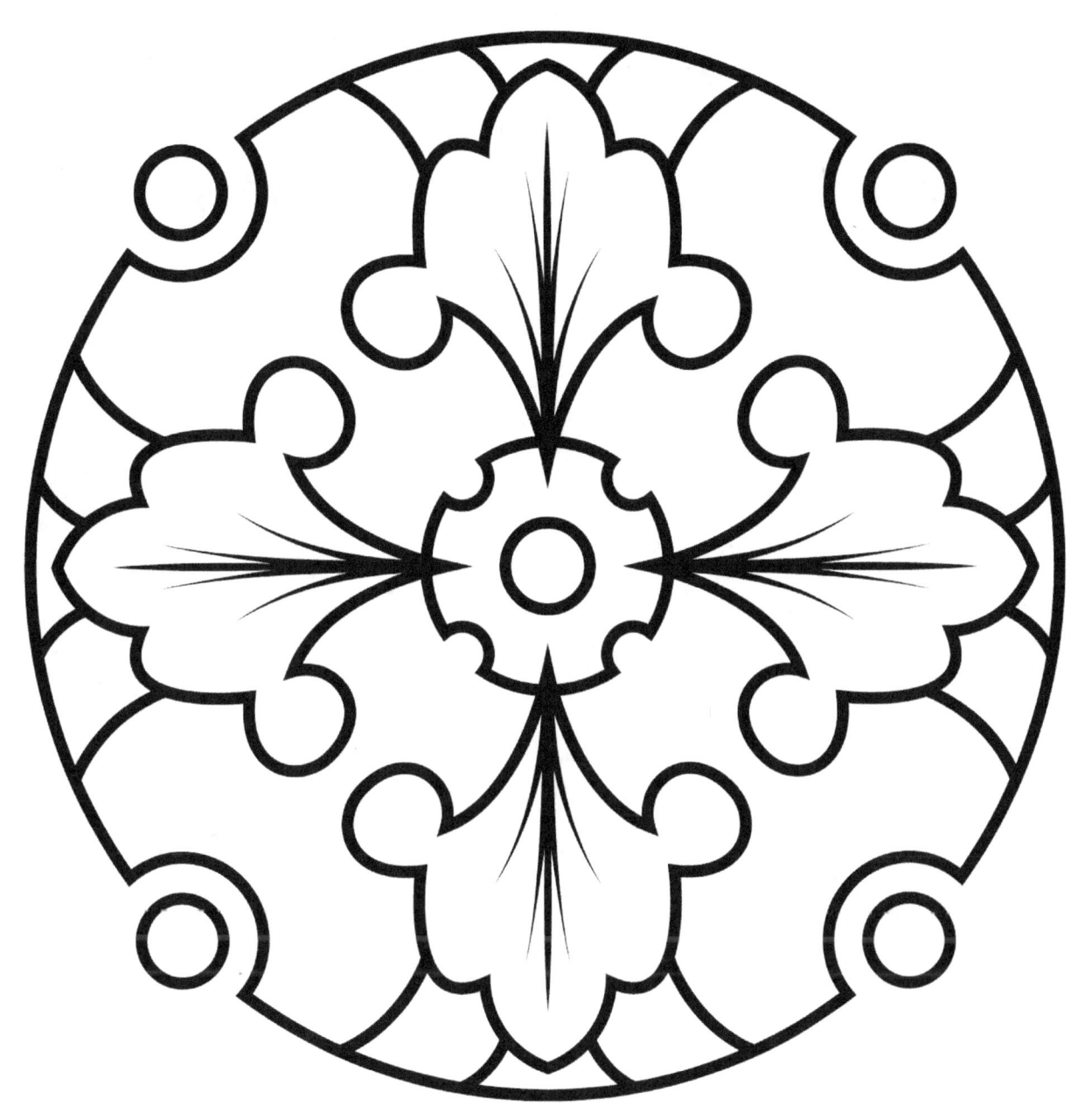

Visualize it and make it be

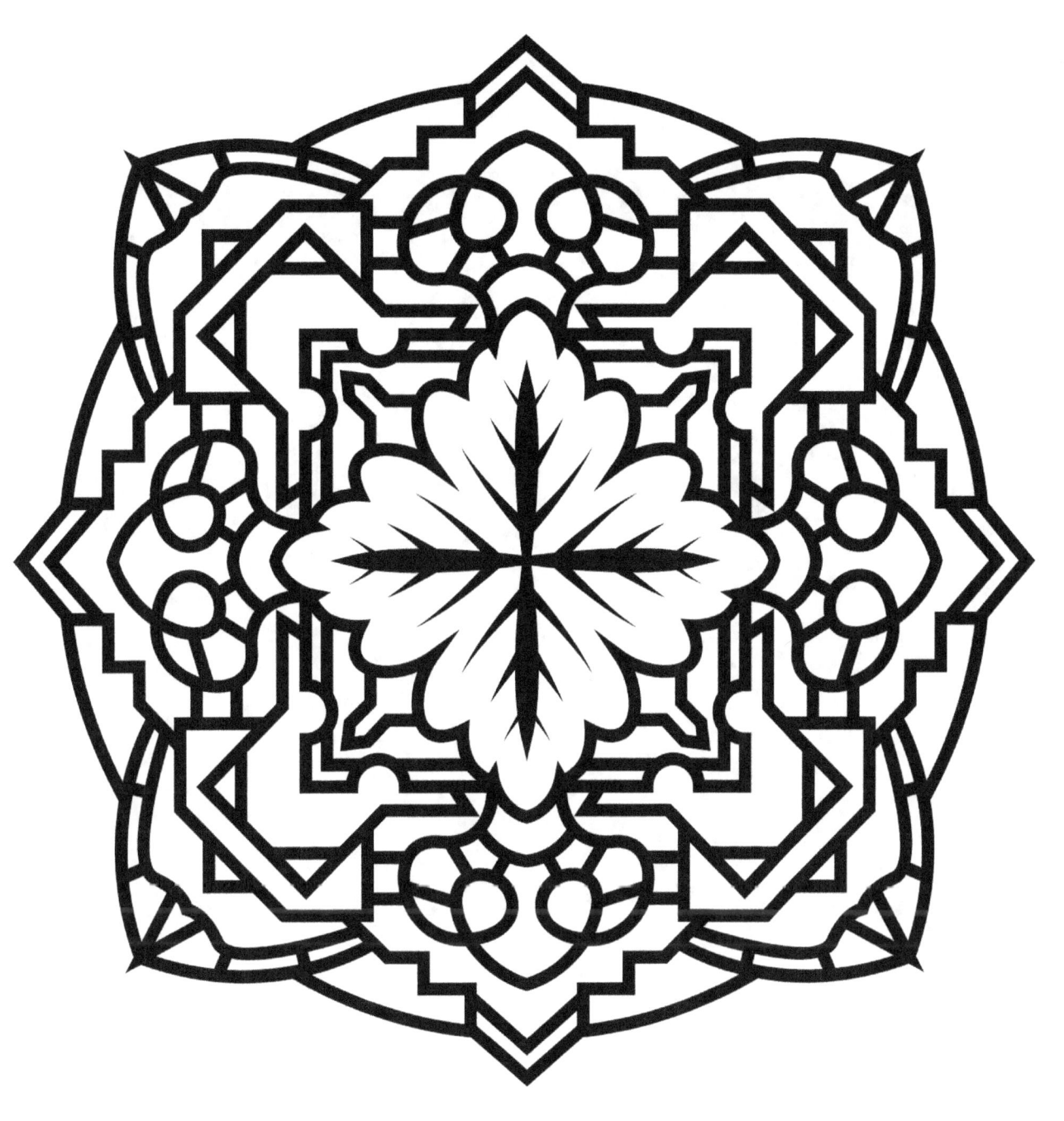

You are beautiful and life is you

ABOUT THE AUTHOR

BinxbyBooks.com is your #1 source for a variety of books for entertainment and organizing your life!

Visit us online at BinxbyBooks.com to learn more and see what we have to offer.

<u>If you enjoyed this book please leave us a review on the site where you ordered it from!</u>

www.ingramcontent.com/pod-product-compliance
Lightning Source LLC
Chambersburg PA
CBHW081442220526
45466CB00008B/2478